Workshops for Teachers:

Becoming Partners for Information Literacy

By Lesley S. J. Farmer

Linworth Publishing, Inc.
Worthington, Ohio

Library of Congress Cataloging-in-Publication Data

Farmer, Lesley S. J.
    Workshops for teachers : becoming partners for information
literacy / by Lesley S. J. Farmer.
        p.   cm. -- (Professional growth series)
    Includes bibliographic references (p. 139).
    ISBN 0-938865-41-2 (paperback)
    1. Library orientation for teachers.   I. Title.   II. Series.
Z711.2.F37 1995
025.5'608'8372--dc20
                                                                   95-1988
                                                                    CIP

Published by Linworth Publishing, Inc.
480 East Wilson Bridge Road, Suite L
Worthington, Ohio 43085

Copyright © 1995 by Linworth Publishing, Inc.

Series Information:
    From The Professional Growth Series

ISBN 0-938865-41-2

5 4 3 2 1

Table of Contents

Acknowledgments

About the Author

Dr. Lesley S. J. Farmer is a Library Media Teacher at Redwood High School in Larkspur, California. She has extensive experience as a school librarian, as a young adult and children's specialist in public libraries, and as a library science instructor, most recently at San Jose State University. Dr. Farmer is the author of a number of articles and books on librarianship.

Linworth Publishing, Inc. would like to thank the following school librarians and teachers for their contributions to *Workshops for Teachers:*

Janet Hofstetter, California High School, California, Missouri
Shelley Glantz, Arlington High School, Arlington, Massachusetts

Section 1
Why Form Partnerships for Information Literacy?

Knowledge is of two kinds: We know a subject ourselves, or we know where we can find information upon it.

Samuel Johnson

It's first period. The teacher brings in a class, who immediately scatter throughout the room. Students stand in line to use the online encyclopedia instead of consulting the three recent hardbound encyclopedia sets. Two students come up to you to ask about the Canary Islands. "There's nothing in the card catalog," they complain. The teacher is working with one student. You notice that he has chosen probably the worst atlas for the topic. The most applicable set of reference tools sits on the shelf, overlooked by the entire class and the teacher; yet you can't get anyone's attention to point them out.

Instead, you are besieged with elementary questions, often the same ones repeatedly. You feel frustrated and undervalued. When you can finally ask the teacher for the assignment handout, he says that because it's in French it would be no use to you. Au contraire!

Does this scene sound familiar?

The Information Age is here, and our students live it every day: on television, in video games, with the computer, with the proliferation of choices that they must confront constantly. While technology abounds to store and retrieve information, data itself seems increasingly fragmented and difficult to grasp.

As librarians, we constantly push for effective intellectual and physical access to information. We know the value and power of information literacy, the *use* of information. Our days are spent teaching students these skills: using CD-ROMs, consulting the *Reader's Guide*, accessing OPACS, interpreting maps. But all too often, we exhaust ourselves answering the same questions repeatedly, one-on-one with students.

As schools increase their use of resource-based education, they too are beginning to see the need for teaching information skills throughout the curriculum. Teachers are using content-rich lessons to challenge students to think critically. Students are engaging themselves as they relate to real-life problems, and solving them by assessing data they collect themselves.

This emphasis on content-embedded information literacy offers the ideal partnership opportunity. Teachers know their curriculum content and their students; librarians know resources and the means to manipulate them.

However, classroom teachers and school librarians too often work in parallel, rather than in tandem.

While we librarians know that planning lessons with teachers should result in higher-level student thinking and higher-quality portfolios, we sometimes run into problems when teachers do not have sufficient information skills themselves. They might not know good research strategies; they might not know what the collection contains; and they might not know how to use a particular resource.

Particularly with the advent of electronic sources, teachers sometimes have no clue how to manipulate the equipment, and don't think they have the time to learn. When such teachers come into the library, they cannot help their students effectively. They may not come at all if they feel embarrassed about not knowing their subject area resources. When uninformed teachers *do* have classes in the library, librarians may bypass the teachers and work only with the students, thus minimizing the long-term educational potential of an information-integrated curriculum.

The need is obvious: Teachers need to become more information literate themselves. Especially when library staffing is limited, trained teachers can plan with librarians to provide information skills opportunities both within the school media center and in the classroom. More students can be taught these skills. The librarian reaches more young people when teachers can act as instructional facilitators.

The obvious question also arises: Why aren't teachers better prepared? Ideally, comprehensive preservice training (e.g., schools of education) should include information literacy, particularly as it applies to resource-based learning. While the American Association of School Librarians of the American Library Association is presently developing information literacy competencies for entry-level teachers, few such requirements now exist for beginning teachers. So inservice training is the sensible vehicle for current teachers to acquire these skills.

Just as it is inefficient (though pleasant) to teach students one by one, so is it inefficient (though sometimes necessary) to instruct teachers individually in information skills. Many are the times that librarians tell how they "converted" or "trained" their teachers one by one. How much more effective to provide workshops for groups of teachers! The librarian can focus information literacy according to grade or content, and allow teachers to interact with one another as well as with the available resources. In fact, when the whole school participates in information literacy opportunities, the result is a stronger climate for learning and wise problem-solving.

This book examines some major issues of information literacy education. The second chapter covers instructional consulting techniques for classroom-based information skills. The third chapter outlines methods of inservice teacher training. The fourth chapter provides tips for more effective workshops. The fifth chapter outlines the workshop framework, and the last section contains sample workshops that school librarians can adapt to meet specific site needs.

Like lesson planning, teacher training requires full cooperative partnership between classroom teachers and school librarians. Their mutual success provides a model for students to emulate and promotes schoolwide commitment to the effective use of ideas and information.

<u>Notes</u>

Section 2

The Librarian as Instructional Consultant

Information Power: Guidelines for School Library Media Programs (ALA and AECT, 1988) lists the following responsibilities of the school librarian as instructional consultant:

- Participating in curriculum design and assessment projects.
- Helping teachers develop instructional activities.
- Providing expertise in materials for the delivery of information and instruction. (p. 35)

Particularly with the acceptance of resource-based and collaborative learning, librarians play an increasingly obvious role in instruction. As we librarians expand our range of responsibilities from warehousing books to providing leadership in the access and use of ideas, we need to reshape our functions.

Concurrently, the role of classroom teachers is changing in response to the growing significance of information literacy. The American Association of School Librarians of the American Library Association is currently developing a set of information skills competencies for educators. They list these:

- Planning and maintaining resource-based learning experiences and environments.
- Structuring information skills and information literacy as an integral part of each subject.
- Using literature as a valid and valuable base for learning in all subject areas.
- Using technology as a tool and resource.

Probably information literacy will be taught in the classroom more than in the library; thus, librarians will need to work more closely with classroom teachers to ensure that they will have adequate skills. This redirection requires pre-assessment of teacher competence, intervention, instruction, and follow-up activity.

Unfortunately, such an instructional leadership role might not be evident to the rest of the school. When bringing students into the library, teachers are often placed in an instructional dilemma. The library is not their home turf. Often they do not frequent the library in their free time. They do not know the collection, even in their own subject areas (although some believe they have a good handle on it). The arrangement of space differs from their classrooms. And they must share the role of authority figure.

What's a teacher to do? Some try to maintain complete control, risking embarassment when they cannot answer the students' informational questions. Some give complete control to the librarian, who likewise risks embarassment if she does not know the teacher's intent or interpretation of the assignment. Some try to learn more about the library, either in the planning process or during the actual library activity.

What's a librarian to do? While workshops may reach the greatest number of teachers, librarians can serve as instructional consultants in other ways as well.

Sharing Instruction

Generally, a school has one library surrounded by dozens of classrooms. Does it make sense that all information literacy instruction must take place in that one center? Particularly when library staffing is limited, trained teachers enable more students to learn and practice valuable information skills. Classroom learning should incorporate information skills anyway, and teachers can make their students accountable for learning.

When conceptualizing information literacy teaching, you can apply the model of reading instruction within the school to the incorporation of "library" skills. Typically, reading skills include:

- Word recognition,
- Vocabulary building,
- The reading process,
- Reading for meaning,
- Interpreting what is read,
- Sharing reading experiences,
- Reading for enjoyment, and
- Information literacy: finding sources and finding facts within a source.

Classroom teachers diagnose student status and ability and guide student progress. They provide a climate for reading and sharing and usually choose the reading material and context for learning.

School librarians complement and reinforce classroom efforts. They too provide a climate for reading (often displaying good books) and promote reading enjoyment through shared reading experiences. Librarians choose and provide a *collection* of reading material and help students select materials from that collection.

Information literacy can thus be couched within the context of reading. Skills associated with information literacy include:

- *Locating:* developing search strategies, using guides such as catalogs and indexes, finding facts within a source (arrangement of sources, reading guides).
- *Evaluating:* main ideas, point of view, content analysis, comparing sources, visual literacy (graphs, pictures).
- *Organizing:* classifying, sequencing, summarizing, symbolizing.
- *Sharing:* written, oral, visual, dramatic or kinesthetic presentation; videotaped, computer-generated, or multimedia production; game.

Following the reading construct, teachers can be considered specialists and librarians generalists. Teachers know their own classes and subject matter in depth. Librarians know students and materials across the curriculum. Thus, teachers are best equipped to concentrate on evaluating information within a source and organizing the results, while librarians would focus on locating information and search strategies.

As team planners assess their own competencies, they can determine who is best qualified to teach each aspect of the lesson. Hopefully, each will learn from the other so both can become better instructors.

Deciding who teaches depends on several other factors as well:

- *Learning objective:* If the emphasis is on specific subject matter, such as invertebrates, teachers usually take control. If the emphasis is on process, such as Boolean searching, librarians typically lead. Ideally, most learning requires both types of skills—and both types of instructors.
- *Location:* Interestingly, educators seem to be tied to place; teachers feel more comfortable within their classroom domain, and librarians prefer teaching in their home base.
- *Resources:* If finding a variety of resources is the objective, probably the librarian will do the instruction. If the emphasis is on the use of a particular resource, such as a specific set of dictionaries, the teacher make help instruct.
- *Product:* While teachers have historically been responsible for guiding students in production of a report or other presentation, librarians increasingly teach production techniques such as videotaping and database development.
- *Assessment:* With written reports, teachers traditionally graded the writing, and the librarian graded the bibliography. As portfolios gain acceptance, team evaluation has become more common. Typically, the teacher grades the content and presentation; the librarian grades the process.

One way to help determine who teaches is to develop a profile of instructional control. During the planning stage, the teacher and librarian mark where along the continuum their involvement lies. A sample is shown here:

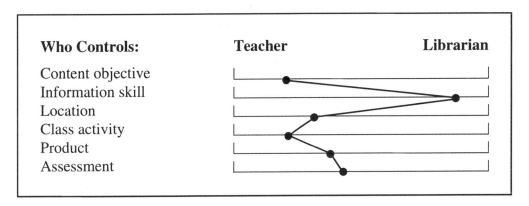

Each area of responsibility may be subdivided, with each person assuming the guiding role for specific aspects. For example, the teacher might explain note-taking in class, and the librarian might teach bibliographic citation skills in the library, both being sure to coordinate the lessons so they incorporate elements the other has taught. For instance, notes should include the bibliographic data that will be needed in the citation.

Once the points on the continuum are determined, a line can be drawn connecting those points to construct a visual profile of team-teaching control.

As students become more skilled, they become more active partners in the instructional process; they assume more control of their learning. The negotiation continuum can be expanded into a triangle, with points graphed to mark the degree of responsibility. Here is a sample graph for an activity in which each student group designs a brochure describing an artistic school or stylistic movement:

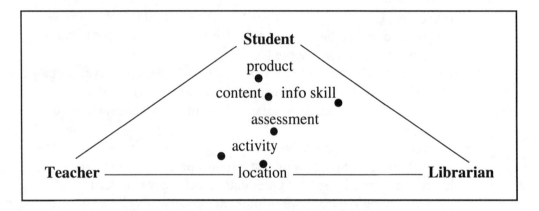

Negotiation occurs on different levels: lesson by lesson, teacher by teacher, grade by grade, subject matter by subject matter. And some points, such as an informational literacy scope and sequence curriculum, can be developed collaboratively by the whole faculty.

Improving Instruction

The process of team-planning and team-teaching provides ample opportunities for librarians to guide teachers towards instructional self-improvement. Like students, teachers learn informational skills best within a meaningful subject context. For the teacher, team-teaching offers personal, customized attention— the best way to gain knowledge.

We librarians unfortunately tend to underplay our natural role as instructional assessors. We watch teachers work with students every day in the library. We have seen the lazy and the incompetent, the practical and the inspiring. We see what works—and what doesn't. As with our cross-curricular view of resources, our observation of teacher performance spans the gamut of competence.

With that knowledge we can take two actions: share good teaching practices with others, and model good strategies ourselves. The latter approach is more subtle. Teachers have the opportunity to watch us and adapt those skills they find helpful without having to expose their own vulnerabilities. As they see what resources we pull out for the students, they learn about the library's collection. Particularly with those teachers who resist criticism or change, modeling effective information strategies is the least offensive way to improve their information literacy. Note that this approach assumes that the teacher be present to make the appropriate observations; thus, we have even greater need for requiring teachers to accompany their classes and to use flexible scheduling.

More direct, and potentially more effective, is active evaluation. As we and the teacher assess a specific library-based activity, we can determine what strategies to use. Did student seating facilitate their activity? Did instruction affect the kind of follow-up assistance students requested? What resources were used? How could instruction or library management be modified to improve student results?

This approach results in dramatic improvement when a teacher has the same assignment for several classes and hasn't planned it with the librarian. By letting the class "happen" the first time and changing instructional methods for ensuing classes, the librarian concretely demonstrates what thoughtful planning can do to improve student outcomes. (The only disadvantage is that the first class suffers because the teacher did not prepare. It is to be hoped that the lesson is effective so the teacher will plan ahead with the librarian for future units.)

Librarians can communicate these success stories to a more general audience. A well-planned and executed project can be shared at a faculty meeting or in a library newsletter. Administrators can hear about effective lessons via monthly reports or casual conversation. Products of team-planning, such as subject bibliographies or "pathways," can be posted on teacher bulletin boards or distributed in campus mail. These informal methods of sharing can sow seeds that germinate into productive learning activities.

Even if we librarians are not part of formal inservice programs, we can act as clearinghouses for information literacy staff development by sharing learning opportunities. Librarians can distribute continuing education announcements, articles on effective information literacy strategies, and results of online searches on information literacy. The goal is to let the school know that librarians care about information literacy and can be valuable resources and consultants on that subject.

Notes

Section 3

Teacher Training

We all know that students won't make the best use of library resources unless they're required to use them across the curriculum. And we know that teachers must be information literate *and* comfortable with the library's resources in order to make assignments that take advantage of those resources.

Presently, inservice training is the most-used formal channel for information literacy teacher education. Such training can be especially effective and accountable when the school is committed to professional development and the importance of library skills. Many states require regular teacher credential updating. Such professional growth should include experiences in polishing information skills that can be transferred to young people.

If a school is just beginning a comprehensive inservice program from scratch, the following steps are important:

1. Develop short-term and long-term goals and objectives within a purposeful program.
2. Generate cooperation and interest among staff.
3. Establish a coordinating structure and policies by which to work.
4. Establish procedures for assessing, designing, and maintaining the program.
5. Design and implement a planned sequence of courses in a variety of delivery modes.
6. Establish training supports: a clearinghouse for information, a professional collection (preferably housed in the library), financial compensation and other recognitions.

A comprehensive, effective inservice program requires much planning and support. While administrative direction is obviously needed, the approach to staff development cannot be construed as a strictly top-down phenomenon. The entire faculty must "buy into" the program. A *needs assessment* completed by staff offers a beginning point for developing meaningful training. This input, together with insights gathered from classroom observations, clarifies the wants and needs that inservice training can address.

Successful inservice programs also require sufficient commitment of *time and money.* Staff development should be a regular budget line item, with money for trainers, support materials, and compensation. Training should be a regular activity, and staff should be allotted follow-up time to practice and incorporate their new skills. Incentive funds should reward staff for improved strategies.

Finally, inservice programs should be an *integrated part of a total school or district effort towards improved education.* Training should not exist in an intellectual vacuum, but should reflect current attitudes towards educational delivery systems. And training results should impact the entire school program, reinforcing a total learning environment.

When we librarians try to incorporate an information-literacy component into staff development, we must keep the above elements in mind. We cannot mandate such training by ourselves. We need to work in concert with other faculty. Sometimes our first task is to raise other people's awareness of their need to improve their information literacy. Next, we must make sure that information literacy is a high priority in the school curriculum; otherwise, no one will see the need for related staff development. Ultimately, we must enlist the support of administration. Without their endorsement, library skills training is an uphill climb.

Adults as Learners

Training adults requires recognition of the special characteristics and needs of mature learners. By addressing these issues, trainers will be more effective, and learners will incorporate inservice experiences more fully.

First, adults are experienced learners. Trainers need to build on those experiences, going from the known to the unknown. Successful training encourages adults to share their prior knowledge and incorporate it into the total training picture. Trainer and trainee should have a reciprocal relationship, each being considered authorities.

Adults have limited time. Therefore, any training must be seen as practical and of immediate use. It should solve some kind of problem for the learner. Training needs to be well-planned and executed so adults will feel that their time is well-spent. Training schedules should also take into account outside, possibly conflicting, adult concerns such as family demands and volunteer or social commitments.

Adults learn in response to their own interests and needs. Training must build on what the learners perceive are their needs. The trainer should establish a climate for learning and then facilitate adult self-improvement. Needs are also physical; trainers should provide breaks and food during training sessions.

Adults have strong habits. They may hear only what they want to hear. To change requires great need. Adults should feel that they can test new skills in a safe environment and that they will be supported in their risk-taking. Their efforts should be compensated through released time, extra pay, increased status, and greater authority. Administrators should support continuing education efforts accordingly.

Adults need to see results. In order to internalize skills, adults need to practice their new learnings, preferably with trainer coaching. Inservice time must include time for adults to plan how to apply their skills, and follow-up contact must be made to ensure practical transfer of learning.

The major task of the trainer is to facilitate change. Change occurs on several levels: personal, organizational, social. The more that inservice training builds on existing structures, providing easy transitions to new practices in a safe learning environment, the more likely that learning will occur. The more that the school organization reinforces change and adopts new practices as the norm, the more likely that learning will be internalized and implemented permanently.

Designing Workshops

The best intentioned inservice program will go awry if it is not meticulously planned and executed. Particularly when the training is library-related, our professional credibility will be on the line; we need to be well-prepared, presenting a convincing and exciting workshop.

Planning a workshop may be considered in four phases: initial decision-making, preparation, implementation, and follow-up. The following tasks and checklist provide a guide to successful workshop results. While this degree of planning is not necessary for small-scale inservices, it offers a broad perspective on training in general.

Determine the need and objectives of the workshop.
  □ Does the workshop fit within the school's goals and objectives?
  □ Has a needs assessment been conducted to determine a good reason for having a workshop?
  □ What are the desired outcomes of the workshop?
  □ Who will take the workshop? Does the workshop fit the level of audience expertise? Does the workshop have application to the targeted audience?
  □ What is the general time frame for planning and implementation?
  □ Who will plan the workshop?
  □ How will the workshop be financed? Some of the possible expenses include content development, trainers, food, duplication, supplies, equipment rental, space rental, and publicity. For most school workshops, the greatest cost will be trainers (unless done in-house) and duplication of materials.

Develop the workshop.
  □ What date should the workshop occur? Check possible conflicting activities.
  □ Where should the workshop take place? Balance the advantages of at-school convenience with possible off-site objectivity. Parking and pubic transportation issues should be addressed. Be sure to check out the site ahead of time for the requisite electric outlets, seating, and lighting.
  □ What should be the time and length of the workshop? To be effective, it should be at least 90 minutes. Decide whether the

workshop will be a one-time session or part of a series. Another alternative is a credit course, which can be developed in conjunction with local higher education institutions.

☐ Who will conduct the workshop? An outside person can provide objective expertise but may lack knowledge about the school culture and needs, and be less effective. One interesting approach is to exchange experts. Librarians can "prep" their colleagues as they ask each other to train their respective faculty. Trainers need to know the audience, the need, the institution, the site, the objectives and outcomes, reimbursements, and any obstacles or factors to consider.

☐ What will be the specific content? The speaker and the planning committee should work together to determine the content. The sequence of events is also important. Possible flow can be ordered by specificity, difficulty, complexity, chronology, age group, theme, or sensitivity or controversy level.

☐ What will be the format? Options include combinations of speech, written, video, computer, and other audiovisual presentations. What accommodations will be made for individual needs? The format should correspond to the content to facilitate transfer of learning.

☐ What resources are needed? Trainers will need equipment. Newsprint and writing tools may be used to record group ideas, for instance. Learners usually expect handouts; duplication needs to be done well ahead of time. You may want to record some sessions on audio- or videotape. Consider workshop folders or bags to hold handouts and name tags.

☐ How will learners be arranged? In theater rows (to facilitate lectures), in a circle (to emphasize equality), or around small tables (to encourage small group interaction)?

☐ How will the workshop be evaluated? Pre- and post-tests, observation, self-assessment, follow-up activities?

☐ How will learning be applied? How will you measure its effects?

☐ What food and beverages will be provided, and by whom? Be sure that needed tables, utensils, containers, and equipment are on hand.

☐ What recognitions or credits will you give, if any?

☐ How will you handle registration? Does the site or type of workshop limit the number of participants? If they are to come from outside the school, you will need procedures for registering and paying for the workshop.

☐ What sponsorship is needed? Will the district be involved? What professional organizations would be interested? Will postsecondary institutions be involved?

☐ Plan for publicity. Even if the workshop is held on campus, staff need to know ahead of time about the training. Flyers or announcements are needed to spread the message. Specifics should include target audience, workshop outcomes, sponsor, time and place, cost, a map or directions, and instructions for registration.

☐ What is the final budget? The number of registrants will affect the cost for handouts, food, and other supplies. Is financial backing sufficient?

One week before the workshop, make sure the following factors are accounted for:
- Responsible people: trainers, registrars, facilitators, volunteer help
- Supplies: writing tools, paper, stands, tape, boards, refreshments
- Resources: videos, exhibits
- Equipment and back-up, bulbs, cords
- Handouts and forms (agenda, registration, evaluation, signage)

Day of the workshop
☐ Who is responsible for set-up, signage, registration, resources, equipment, refreshments, hostessing, distribution, parking, clean-up?
☐ During training who will distribute handouts, check on equipment, hand out and collect evaluation forms?

Follow-up
☐ Has everyone been thanked?
☐ Have equipment and other materials been returned?
☐ Has a participants' list been developed and distributed?
☐ Are all bills paid?
☐ Have evaluation forms been tallied, interpreted, and acted upon?

Conducting Workshops

Probably the most important aspect of a workshop is its tone and climate. Participants should feel comfortable and eager to learn. The presenters should be organized and enthusiastic. The room should be pleasant and equipped. A well-designed program begun on time with a warm welcome and clear direction sets the stage for workshop success. Including question time and opportunities to share information ensure engagement and satisfaction. Ending on time and closing with an inspiring call to action make for a satisfying end to a worthwhile workshop.

The workshop itself should take adult education principles into account as well as the course content. Experiential learning is probably the most effective means of learning for adults. This model assumes that a person engages in some activity, reflects upon and generalizes from it, then applies it to daily life. The following five-point model describes the sequence of activities for an experiential learning workshop:
- Experiencing (activity, doing, data-gathering)
- Sharing reactions and observations (data processing)
- Processing by discussing patterns and dynamics
- Generalizing by inferring principles about the real world (the "so what?" stage)
- Applying skills and planning more effective behavior. "Where do we go from here?"

Teamwork is important, particularly when hands-on activity or group input comprise part of the workshop. Working in small groups combines cognitive and affective learning and stimulates thinking and insights. Peer acceptance of new ideas is easier than obedience to a superior's directive. Follow-up can be more effective, too, as small group interaction establishes informal network groups.

Some specific activities are well suited to small group work: discussion, problem-solving, case study, and brainstorming. In each case, different options are raised and considered so that sources for decision-making can be increased.

Managing small groups requires clear directions and time frames. In addition, each group needs to have assigned roles, at least of facilitator and record-keeper. At the end of any small group activity, there should be an opportunity for each group to report its findings and for group members to incorporate insights into the total group process.

Workshops also possess a type of rhythm or flow. Activities generally follow this sequence:

- *Early-bird activity:* Early participants need to feel involved from the start. Have handouts for them to read, food as a socializing focus, last-minute preparation tasks that they can help with.

- *Introduction:* The facilitator or leading speaker should introduce major presenters and agenda and announce "housekeeping" details.

- *Warm-up:* The group needs to get acquainted with each other and the speaker. Sharing backgrounds and expectations helps focus participants.

- *Definition:* The facilitator needs to explain the main concepts and their significance.

- *Main activities:* The heart of the workshop should model the main ideas and allow the facilitator to check for group understanding.

- *Practice and application:* The group should practice and reflect on the concepts or skills presented. Participants should have the opportunity to plan ways to transfer their learning to their own educational setting.

- *Resources:* The group should have the materials needed to implement their learning. Bibliographies, resource people, and readings offer ways for participants to pursue the topic on their own.

- *Closing:* The group needs a sense of closure. The main findings should be summarized, and follow-up strategies should be outlined. Participants should evaluate the workshop before leaving, although later follow-up contact can measure longer-term transfer of learning.

Evaluating Workshops

Learning can be assessed on several levels. Both trainer and trainee can assess the quality and usefulness of a workshop; in fact, evaluation time must be built into the session's schedule. However, the real evaluation is the effect that the workshop has on student learning. This effect is harder to measure, for a comparison control group rarely exists. Factors to consider in evaluation include attitudinal differences, test results, and levels of intellectual and affective engagement. Measurement tools can include observations, objective and standardized tests, teacher and student "products," portfolio assessments, clinical supervision, peer- and self-assessments, and focus group discussion.

Evaluation is the key: Knowing what worked and what didn't, and why, can help you modify the content or the approach to better meet everyone's needs. Some factors to assess include:

- *Content:* level of difficulty, balance of theory and practice, level of usefulness
- *Delivery:* format, pacing, sequence, clarity
- *Time:* date, time of day, length of workshop, breaks
- *Space:* size, arrangement, seating, physical conditions
- *Resources:* handouts, teaching aids, equipment (each considered in terms of quality and quantity)

One particularly good question to ask workshop attendees is "What do you want to learn now, as a result of today's training?" Their response provides direction for future programs. The subsequent workshop can then relate to the first one, either building on it or complementing it. For example, a storytelling workshop could lead into student activities following shared reading, or it could lead to the study of myths across the curriculum.

Hopefully, your first workshop will have your teachers begging for more! Ideally, a staff development committee should plan a logical series of related inservice workshops so faculty can progress systematically throughout the year. Often, inservice workshops are developed one by one in response to immediate needs. Whether yours is ad hoc or part of a continuum, the first inservice is pivotal, for its outcome will help determine whether you will have the support necessary to offer similar sessions in the future.

<u>Notes</u>

Section 4

Training Tips

Like classroom teaching, inservice training is both a science and an art. Beyond the basic skills of designing and delivering the workshop, you will be more successful and have more fun when you can dip into a repertoire of training "tricks" to spice up the session. This chapter covers typical situations that call for extra attention. The following topics will be covered; use them as a checklist when developing workshops:
  • Communication tips
  • Warm-up activities
  • Selecting training presentation aides
  • Selecting training methods
  • Group structure
  • Facilitating small group work
  • Techniques for applying learning to the classroom
  • Team-training
  • Conference tips

Communication Tips

Although content is the basis of a workshop, and participation is its heart, personal delivery greatly affects the workshop's outcome. Even before you open your mouth, the ability to train is being judged, based on appearance:
  • Are you on time?
  • Do you look calm and prepared, not haggard or rushed?
  • Are you dressed professionally?
  • Are you warm and cordial to everyone?

Such details count. While speaking, use good oral presentation habits:
• Talk clearly, loudly, and distinctly.
• Relay enthusiasm and warmth through your voice.
• Modulate the tone without becoming sing-songy.
• Talk in a relaxed and natural way, and try not to rush (an unconscious habit when we feel stressed).
• Use gestures only for emphasis. Unconscious practices such as waving your arms or touching your hair can be distracting.

A valuable, though possibly uncomfortable, exercise is to prepare the presentation in front of a mirror with a tape recorder. Having a friend videotape you in a practice session can also clue you to potentially distracting mannerisms.

As you train, use visuals. Either distribute an outline of the training for the audience to follow, or write the main points as you introduce them. An overhead works best because you can maintain eye contact with the group. (Tip: turn off the projector when you're not using it so people will know not to keep their attention on the screen.) A pad of newsprint sheets on an easel is also effective because sheets can be posted once they're filled. (Another tip: alternate pen color between lines to make the print easier to read.)

One final note about equipment: Be prepared! A bulb may burn out, a computer projection system may not be compatible with your computer port, a slide projector may get stuck. If possible, have a back-up system so your presentation won't be "shot" if something goes wrong.

Warm-up Activities

Building a climate for learning requires that trainees be comfortable so they can concentrate on the topic at hand. A vital part of that process involves getting to know one another: trainee to trainee, and trainee to trainer. If the workshop is done in-house where everyone knows each other, an atmosphere-setting opener can energize the group. In either case, the warm-up demonstrates your style of training and the type of content to expect. Here are some sample "ice-breaker" activities:

Group census: Ask the group to raise their hands if a statement applies to them. For example: specify grade level, years taught, frequency of library use.

Bingo: Create a 3x3 to 5x5 bingo card, filling in each square with some aspect of the inservice. For example, a storytelling workshop might generate the following bingo card:

Attended a storytelling workshop	Told a story to my class	Enjoy hearing stories
Tell stories to my own children	Listened to stories as a child	Used a prop when telling a story
Know a story to tell	Like to read stories	Know a storyteller

Participants go around the room, collecting names of people to fill in the bingo squares. The object of the activity is to either be the first to fill the card or make a Bingo line, or to have the entire group fill the card or make a Bingo line.

Mix and Mingle: Provide a sheet of sentences to complete and have each person find different people to finish each sentence. For a workshop on reference tools, sentences can act as a pre-test (e.g., "The name of one magazine index is . . . "; "A good place to find maps is . . . "; "Census figures can be found in . . . ").

Interviews: Divide the group into pairs and have them interview each other about their prior experiences with the workshop topic, such as the use of poetry in their classroom.

Drawing: Have each person draw the ideal student and share the drawing with their neighbor.

Memory lane: In pairs, have participants share their own school library experiences as teenagers.

What if?: Pose a controversial question that counters most assumptions, such as "What if there were no libraries?" Have pairs discuss the ramifications.

Game time: Have the group play a trivia facts or concentration game that builds on the workshop topic. (This is often a good sample classroom activity, to be introduced later in the workshop.)

Sign boards: Each person makes a sign board that completes sentences, such as "I like students who . . . ," "My greatest teaching experience was . . . ," "One famous person I would like as a teacher is . . . ." Have the group go around the room examining each other's signs.

Matching cards: Ahead of time, write two-part index cards with questions and answers on the workshop topic, such as a reference question and answer or source. Cut the cards between question and answer, making a jagged line, and mix the sets. At the beginning of the workshop, hand a card to each participant. At the cue, have them find their "mate" and sit with that person. This activity mixes up participants so they will work with different people than they would normally sit beside.

Selecting Training Presentation Aids

A variety of aids can help you make your point more clearly. The following list describes advantages and disadvantages of a number of training aids. As you consider training aids, think about the audience, available equipment, room set-up, purpose of the aid, and appropriateness of the medium to the message.

Transparencies allow the audience to see main points, both in text and in picture. Transparencies are easy to prepare and flexible to use. Be sure that the print is large enough for everyone to see. Include color or graphics whenever possible to liven up the presentation.

Charts provide graphic representation of facts. To carry the message, they must be simple, colorful, and clear.

Displays allow viewers to see the main idea immediately and examine content at their own pace. Displays serve as motivators, learning stations, and attraction centers.

Videotapes provide information in "real time" motion. In-house productions offer customized perspectives that might be otherwise hard to see, such as a class demonstration. Videotapes are particularly effective as objective feedback about teacher behavior. Two cautionary notes: Make sure the camera and editing quality are high and make sure everyone can see the video monitor clearly.

Slide-tape presentations require considerable preparation, but they pay off in showing custom pictures and sound. Slides are portable and flexible so they can be rearranged for different purposes. Note that most slide shows require a darkened room.

Computer multimedia offers an interactive setting for learning, combining sound, action, graphics, and text. Material can be customized and attractively presented. The drawback is the time it takes to product a high quality multimedia presentation. Two other drawbacks are possible breakdown of any component and difficulty in staging the presentation so that everyone in the audience can see all parts of it.

Selecting Training Methods

Information can be imparted in a variety of ways. As with training aids, methods should be chosen based on audience, desired outcomes, skill of the trainer, time frame (including preparation time available), space, and appropriateness to the content.

Presentations constitute the traditional way to provide information and the method most trainers rely on. Specific techniques include lecture, panel (different points of view), debate (encourages polarization), and introductory audiovisual shows.

Demonstrations model "correct" techniques or processes. To be effective, they should be followed by an opportunity for trainees to practice the skills demonstrated.

Dramatizations simulate situations and involve emotional as well as intellectual learning. Trainees become involved when they role-play situations.

Case studies provide realistic situations that require problem-solving. They encourage transfer of knowledge to specific application. Good case studies emphasize process as much as result.

Games and simulations give information and immediate feedback, facilitate decision-making and problem-solving, increase interest, and link to reality. Some adults may react negatively to "cutesy" games so choose exercises carefully.

Group Structures

Research shows that the most effective learning occurs in small groups. People tend to participate more because they risk less when speaking to a few others, yet they are more accountable because their behavior is more likely to be noticed. In addition, people tend to be more committed to a small number of peers, so will be more likely to follow up on the training.

Experience shows that the most effective small group size is five to six, large enough to elicit a variety of responses but small enough to stay cohesive. Experience also shows that a tight circle is the most effective seating arrangement. While tables are useful for writing on, they can act as communication barriers.

Groups can be structured in several ways, depending on training objectives. The trainer's role is dictated by each arrangement, so the deciding factor in group structure should be the training outcomes desired.

Task groups are used to solve specific problems. The trainer is usually outside of the group, acting as an observer and consultant, as needed. This structure is rarely used for inservice workshops.

Discussion groups allow members to talk freely about some important topic. A free flow of ideas and feelings occurs in this structure. The trainer intervenes mainly to activate and end the discussion.

Brainstorming groups elicit and prioritize ideas. They can accommodate a larger size than other structures. The trainer keeps the group moving from generating ideas, to clarifying them, to prioritizing them. The trainer should *not* editorialize.

Tutorial groups teach members specific skills. The trainer can instruct the entire group in lecture form, but the more effective method is individual coaching.

Explorer groups develop learner skills by asking questions leading to a thorough exploration of a topic. The learners ask the trainer questions to help them understand the information they are exploring.

Facilitating Small Group Work

A small group facilitates the sharing of ideas and also helps people solve problems through interactive thinking. In a small group, people are more likely to test ideas and work them through, clarifying and evaluating them in the process. At its most basic, a small group can encourage individual participation, *but only if it is well directed.*

The trainer optimizes learning conditions by:
- Assigning people to groups
- Explaining the group task: what to accomplish, how to accomplish it, and in what time frame to accomplish it
- Clarifying member roles
- Checking for clarity and quality of work
- Summarizing and giving closure

Within the group, each person plays a role, minimally as a participant (both speaking and listening actively). Usually for workshop groups, only two or three specific roles are needed: leader or facilitator, recorder, and reporter. The job of the leader is to get the discussion started, keep the group on task, make sure everyone participates equitably, and finish on time. The recorder writes down the group's ideas and organizes them, and the reporter shares the group's ideas with the larger group. Typically, the group members, rather than the trainer, choose who will carry out the roles.

Techniques for Applying Learning to the Classroom

Every workshop should include a "call to action": some follow-up task that the participants will do. For real transfer of learning, participants need to practice their skills, plan how to incorporate them into their work, and be held accountable for applying their skills.

During the workshop attendees can test the application of ideas by role-playing, acting as students in directed activities, and assessing their skills.

Ideally, participants should draw up action plans, with clear steps for applying their skills. If a copy of those plans is made, the participant can keep one copy and another faculty member (peer, supervisor, administrator) can keep the other copy for follow-up assessment.

Follow-up is essential. Buddies can keep tabs on each other; departments can discuss problems and solutions of applying skills; clinical supervision can focus on the application of workshop skills.

Team Training

Training by yourself can be easier; you have complete control of the process. However, team-training enriches the presentation since two people can share ideas and responsibilities for content and delivery. The ideal team is a librarian and a classroom teacher, because they model true curriculum partnership.

Team-training, however, requires extra time for planning. Who will be responsible for each activity? How will training styles mesh or complement each other? How will follow-up be divided? Team-training works best when the two trainers have established a strong, positive working partnership in day-to-day operations. This professional relationship facilitates workshop planning and has the added benefit of presenting a credible image to the trainees.

Conference Tips

If you are fortunate enough to present at a conference, a few extra pointers will help you prepare accordingly.

The most important piece of advice is: check with the conference planners. They arrange rooms and provide needed equipment and supplies. They can limit the number of workshop attendees so you can plan presentation styles better. They can arrange seating to accommodate the type of workshop, be it lecture or small group work. Given enough lead time, they can often duplicate and deliver handout materials too. Plan ahead, though, for sometimes requests for machines have to be made several months ahead.

On the day of the workshop, try to check the room ahead of time. Find out if equipment and supplies are ready. Get comfortable with the room's atmosphere, and locate any outlets and PA system you might need. If you have a backup plan, you can make adjustments in time. For example, handouts might not arrive; keep a master copy of each sheet, and locate the nearest photocopy service to the conference site. Computers might not be compatible with your software; having a few transparencies handy just in case will save you embarrassment.

Get to the room a few minutes before the workshop to set up—and psyche up. Other people may be available to help distribute handouts or get supplies in order. Often someone will introduce you; have a one-page fact sheet about yourself to hand them so they will feel comfortable presenting you.

Another difference between a school-site workshop and a conference session is the audience: most people will be strangers, and often the number of attendees is a mystery right up to the moment of delivery. While you have an idea of the approximate background of attendees, do a quick hand count at the beginning of the workshop (e.g., how many represent each type of library, or who teach at a particular grade level). That way, you can make slight adjustments in your workshop to fit the needs of that specific audience. Thus, it is a good idea to have a good repertoire of example to choose from to match your audience's interests; if, for example, you find yourself talking mainly to elementary librarians instead of senior high specialists, you should be prepared to cite age-appropriate books as needed.

Questions may arise during the workshop. Usually it is harder to address each person's concern throughout the session and keep on track. One compromise is to distribute index cards to the audience at the beginning of the workshop, and encourage them to jot down questions as they arise. Have assistants gather the cards near the end of the formal presentation so you can go through the cards and address queries to the whole group. When the workshop is over, people may then come up to speak with you about particular issues. Have your business card available as well so people can contact you at a more convenient time.

Follow-up is more difficult with conference workshops. Instead, encourage attendees to "buddy-up" with each other to reinforce their learning. Sometimes conference planners distribute a list of attendees. One informal way to facilitate exchanges is to have each attendee write their name and telephone number on a sheet of paper, then make a paper airplane or satellite (wadded paper) with the sheet, and throw it; each person should get one missile. If you have the group jot down a joint date in their personal calendars, each person can contact the other then.

Conference workshops may entail more work than school-site sessions, but they serve as an important means to share insights. Especially when librarians address related groups, such as reading teachers or administrators, we send a broadcast message about the significance of library media centers and their staff.

Section 5

Workshop Framework

This section provides an information literacy inservice workshop framework and generic planning and evaluation forms. Transcending rote instruction, the framework emphasizes creative, critical uses of information. It is the basic structure for the 14 workshops in the section that follows.

It is flexible enough to use in introducing different skills at different age levels and adapting workshops for other grades. You may use it to modify an existing workshop as well as to develop original workshops.

<u>Notes</u>

Workshop Framework

Title of workshop	State the major focus of the session.
Intended audience	Identify the most appropriate grade level or subject area teachers and administrators for the workshop.
Objectives	What teachers should accomplish as a result of this workshop.
Set-up	Include here everything the trainer needs to know to plan, organize, and conduct the workshop: group format, equipment and supply needs, additional help (e.g., small group facilitators).
Workshop overview	Summarize the sequence of activities—what will happen and how long it will take.
Content	*Early bird activity*
	Introduction
	Rationale for skill
	Sample skill activities
	Resources
	Lesson planning
	Application
	Wrap-up
	Go into detail on each of the above. Include the trainer's instructions to the audience, at least in outline form. Note the strategy and resources to be used for each part of the workshop.
Resources	Handouts, bibliographies, and other learning aids.
Evaluation	How will the trainer check for understanding and determine whether learners will be able to apply their skills independently? Provide for participants to evaluate the workshop, and include follow-up assessment.
Variations	How can the workshop be modified to fit different audiences or time frames?
Additional information	Identify related skills and applications.

Teacher-Librarian Planning Process

1. Define your objectives: _____
   Content objective(s): _____
   _____

   Informational skills objective(s): _____
   _____
   _____

2. Define your learners:
   Prerequisite learning: _____

   Present level: _____
   _____
   _____

3. Design your activity:
   How will responsibility be divided? _____
   _____

   Where will the activity occur? _____
   _____

   What concepts or information will be presented? _____
   _____

   What resources will be used? _____
   _____

   How will the material be presented? _____
   _____

   How will it be sequenced? _____
   _____

   What is the time frame? _____
   _____

   What learning reinforcement will be provided? _____
   _____

   How will learners be grouped? _____
   _____

   How will instruction be individualized? _____
   _____

   How will learning be applied? _____
   _____
   _____

4. Design your assessment:
   How will you evaluate the learning? _____
   _____

   How will you evaluate the instruction? _____
   _____
   _____
   _____

Workshop Evaluation Form

Title _____ Date _____

Rate the following aspects of this workshop in terms of presentation quality, your interest, and applicability (4 being "excellent," 3 being "good," 2 being "adequate," 1 being "needs improvement"):

Topic	Quality	Interest	Use
Sample activities	4 3 2 1	4 3 2 1	4 3 2 1
Resources	4 3 2 1	4 3 2 1	4 3 2 1
Small group planning	4 3 2 1	4 3 2 1	4 3 2 1
Arrangements	4 3 2 1	4 3 2 1	4 3 2 1

Complete the following:

One part of the workshop that I especially liked was _____
_____
_____
_____
_____

One activity I plan to do as a result of this workshop is _____
_____
_____
_____
_____

One way I would improve this workshop is _____
_____
_____
_____
_____

As a result of this workshop, I now want to know _____
_____
_____
_____
_____

Other comments:
_____
_____
_____
_____
_____
_____

Thank you for making the next workshop even more successful!

<u>Notes</u>

Section 6

Sample Workshops

The 14 workshops in this section follow the framework outlined in Section 5. An asterisk (*) following a name or item means that a sample or handout may be found in the pages at the end of the workshop.

1. Personalizing the Curriculum Through Biographies
2. Fun and Games in Information Literacy
3. Expanding the Story Hour Experience
4. The Magic of Poetry
5. Looking with the Inner Eye: Appreciating Illustration
6. Arithmetic Through Reading
7. Beyond Book Reports
8. Myth and Legend Across the Curriculum
9. Mapping the World
10. Creating and Using Databases
11. The Research Process
12. Exploring Careers Across the Curriculum
13. Curriculum by the Numbers: Using Statistical Sources
14. Encouraging Your Child to Read

<u>Notes</u>

Personalizing the Curriculum Through Biographies

Intended audience   High school teachers across the curriculum.

Objectives   Teachers will
- List ways that biographies can enrich their curriculum.
- Identify biographies that relate to their curriculum.
- Incorporate biographies into their curriculum.

Set-up   If the workshop is held in the library, teachers can consult the library catalog and browse the shelves for interesting biographies. Be sure to give teachers the opportunity to borrow interesting titles. Arrange teachers in small groups by subject area for guided practice. Use a large newsprint pad on an easel or an overhead projector to present ideas. Each group should have newsprint to "publish" its lesson plan and writing materials to make notes.

Workshop overview

125 minutes

Introduction:	Welcome, housekeeping details, directions	10
Rationale:	Contributions to the field	
	Why use biographies?	15
Sample activities:	Picture these booktalks	10
	Biography resume	15
	Group processing	10
Break:		10
Resources:	Bibliography and group titles	10
Lesson planning:	Model teacher-librarian planning	5
Application:	Small groups plan lesson and report out	30
Wrap-up:	Summary, evaluation, follow-up	10

Content   *Early bird activity:* Display biographies for teachers to examine. Give teachers an autobiography crossword puzzle* to complete.

Introduction: Post the agenda and state the goals clearly so teachers will know what to expect. Emphasize resource-based learning and teacher-librarian collaboration.

Rationale for skill: In small groups arranged by subject area, have teachers list famous people in their field and discuss how each famous person relates to the curriculum. Have each group report out on one contributor to the field. Record their findings.

Next, *define biographies.* Show a couple of biography books. State the use of biographies in the curriculum: "Biographies make learning come alive and assume a personal connection. Biographies also affirm each individual's ability to make a difference—a powerful message for youth self-esteem. Biographies are often dramatic stories, as well, that appeal to the reader's emotions. Because they are 'people on paper,' biographies can breathe life into subject matter. In addition, students can use critical-thinking skills to assess how individual contributions were achieved."

Sample skill activities: Begin this section by saying, "Let's see how biographies can be used in interesting ways throughout the curriculum. You have already received one biography-related activity sheet—a crossword puzzle. Now we're going to do a couple of activities that you might want to try in your classroom. As we work through these exercises, I want you to reflect on these questions:
• What did you learn about each famous person?
• How did the activity facilitate learning?
• How can biographies be used for each discipline?

Feel free to make comments after each activity, or wait until this portion of the workshop is completed."

Picture these booktalks: Describe a critical event in a famous person's life, preferably as he or she was growing up, without supplying the person's name. For example, tell how a young boy's chemical experiments resulted in setting a train baggage car on fire. (*World Book* gives good examples of youthful incidents in the lives of famous people.) Show a picture of the person, preferably at the time of the incident, and have the group identify the person (in the above example, Edison). Booktalk a few biography titles in this manner.

Write a famous resume: With the whole group, create a resume for a famous person such as Abraham Lincoln. If there is enough time and interest, have pairs of teachers create resumes of subjects of their choice.

Processing: Divide the teachers into two groups; assign one the booktalk activity, the other the resume. Have each group reflect on their assigned activity by answering the questions posed at the start of the session. Have each group report their conclusions.

Break: Announce that this time might be well spent examining book displays and biography shelves, since the next activity will be to construct a resource list of useful biography titles.

Resources: Hand out a sample bibliography of biographies for potential use in the classroom. A valuable source is the American Library Association's *Biographies for the College Bound.* Show some lesser known titles and suggest ways to use them in the classroom. Good "prospects" are rite-of-passage books, local personalities, memoirs, autobiographies, and people identified with a certain era, school, or movement, such as Andy Warhol.

As a large group, create a longer list of titles. Alternatively, teachers may want to divide into small groups by subject area to develop curriculum-specific bibliographies. In either case, use the standard brainstorm process:
• Elicit responses from individuals in turn.
• Record each title for all to see.
• Allow comments only for clarification; no judgments.
• Ask for clarification as needed.

These lists may be typed and distributed as a follow-up handout.

Lesson planning: Using an item from the Idea Starters* handout and the Teacher-Librarian Lesson Planning Process* handout from Section 5, walk the group through the teacher-librarian planning process.

Application: Divide the group into thirds and have them use the Teacher-Librarian Lesson Planning Process* handout to plan a lesson. At this time, distribute the Idea Starters* handout or give each teacher a good biography as a starting point. The groups may want to brainstorm a number of activities, but they should plan one activity in detail. Give them five minutes to summarize and record their plan and discuss the process they followed. They will then report to the large group. The resulting records may be typed up and distributed as a follow-up handout.

Wrap-up: Summarize insights that the group gained from incorporating biographies into the curriculum. Provide a direction for pursuing library-related activities using biographies. Each teacher should walk away with at least one usable idea.

Be sure the group is given at least five minutes to evaluate the workshop. This helps in planning future workshops.

In closing, thank all the facilitators and participants.

Resources Annotated bibliographies of biographies held by the library. Other useful resources include

Dennenberg, Dennis, and Lorraine Roscoe, *American Historical Fiction and Biography for Children and Young People.* Metuchen NJ: Scarecrow, 1994.

Flack, Jerry D., *Lives of Promise: Studies in Biography and Family History.* Englewood CO: Libraries Unlimited, 1992.

Hartman, Donald, and Gregg Sapp, *Historical Figures in Fiction.* Phoenix: Oryx, 1994.

Reese, Lyn, and Jean Wilkinson, Eds., *Women in the World*. Metuchen NJ: Scarecrow, 1987.

Rochman, Hazel, *Against Borders*. Chicago: American Library Association, 1993.

Evaluation

Each small group shares one lesson plan incorporating biographies. Their ideas may be typed up for follow-up distribution. By the end of the quarter teachers will share, in a departmental or faculty meeting, one lesson they taught that incorporated biographies. The librarian may write up the best librarian-teacher-produced lesson plans for school publications.

Variations

- Focus on one type of biography: fictionalized, autobiography, early lives of famous people.
- Focus on one subject area. Customize the workshop for each department.
- Modify sample classroom activities for younger grades.

Additional information

This workshop reinforces resource-based learning. Fictional works poetry, and drama can also be used to engage student imagination. Biographical information can also be culled from reference sources, thus incorporating research strategies.

Autobiography Crossword Puzzle

Name the authors:

Across

3. *Changing*
8. *With a Voice To Sing With*
9. *Go East, Young Man*
10. *Bring Me a Unicorn*
14. *Me Me Me Me Me*
15. *Palm Sunday*
17. *Out on a Limb*
20. *Will There Really Be a Morning?*
21. *The Greatest*
22. *One More Time*
23. *A Time to Heal*
25. *The Camera Never Blinks*
26. *Ball Four*

Down

1. *My Life on the Plains*
2. *Life Among the Savages*
4. *Self-Consciousness*
5. *Blackberry Winter*
6. *Paper Lion*
7. *Days of Grace*
8. *My Several Worlds*
11. *An American Childhood*
12. *This I Remember*
13. *Boston Boy*
16. *Death Be Not Proud*
18. *I Know Why the Caged Bird Sings*
19. *Growing Up*
22. *Knock Wood*
24. *Act One*

Autobiography Crossword Key

Across	Down
3. Ullman	1. Custer
8. Baez	2. Jackson
9. Douglas	4. Updike
10. Lindbergh	5. Mead
14. Kerr	6. Plimpton
15. Vonnegut	7. Ashe
17. Maclaine	8. Buck
20. Farmer	11. Dillard
21. Ali	12. Roosevelt
22. Burnett	13. Hentoff
23. Ford	16. Gunther
25. Rather	18. Angelou
26. Bouton	19. Baker
	22. Bergen
	24. Hart

Idea Starters

Ten Student Projects:

Dress up as a famous person and speak of firsthand experiences.

Develop a panel of contemporaneous people such as Abraham Lincoln, Stephen Douglas, Frederick Douglass, Jefferson Davis, and Harriet Beecher Stowe. Role-play their interaction.

Use puppets or stick figures to dramatize a person's life.

Create "Twenty Questions" about a famous person.

"Spin" biographical information into a mystery format and reveal the solution through a booktalk presentation. This is very good for inventors and discoverers.

Using "trivia" facts about a famous person, create a game format.

Create a resume for a famous person.

Create an Academy Awards simulation for leading contributors to a field (e.g., scientists, artists, composers).

Write an epic poem about a famous person.

Make a collage about a famous person.

Notes

Fun and Games in Information Literacy

Intended audience	School teachers across the curriculum.

Objectives

Teachers will
- List ways that games can be used to teach information skills.
- Identify resources that can be transformed into games.
- Incorporate games into information skills learning.

Set-up

Arrange teachers in small groups by subject area for guided practice. Spread game books and game boards on the tables. Have fact books such as almanacs available for guided practice.

Reminder: Read the sample activities to prepare needed materials ahead of time. Use a large newsprint pad on an easel and felt markers or an overhead transparency projector to present ideas. Each group should have newsprint to "publish" its lesson plan and writing materials to make notes.

Workshop overview

160 minutes

Introduction:	Welcome, housekeeping details, directions	10
Rationale:	Contributions to the field	
	Why use games?	15
Sample activities:	Authors*	10
	Sequences	10
	Get on board!*	15
	Group processing	10
Break:		10
Resources:	Bibliography and group titles	15
Lesson planning:	Model teacher-librarian planning	10
Application:	Small groups plan lesson and report out	40
Wrap-up:	Summary, evaluation, follow-up	15

Content

Early bird activity: Hand out Categories* activity sheet. Display game books and board games on tables for teachers to browse.

Introduction: Post the agenda and state the goals clearly so teachers will know what to expect. Emphasize resource-based learning and teacher-librarian collaboration.

Rationale for skill: Begin the workshop by drawing out teachers' personal experiences with games in general and within instructional settings. Have them share their thoughts in pairs, then report them to the larger group. Synthesize their findings. Identify categories of games, such as

- Word (Categories, crossword puzzles),
- Cards (Concentration, rummy),
- Board (circle, path),
- Observation,
- Action (charades, ball), and
- Learning station round-robin.

State the case for using games to teach information literacy by saying, "Games offer opportunities for all types of cooperative and interactive learning. Their format motivates and intrigues students and encourages reality-based problem-solving. Teachers can use games to teach and review facts. Students can create games as a culminating activity that can be used in future classes as an introduction."

Within small heterogeneous groups have teachers brainstorm the kinds of information or concepts that can be adapted to a games format. As each group reports its ideas, have the large group suggest what kind of game could be appropriate.

Offer guidelines on designing curriculum-related games, writing the checklist on newsprint or overhead transparency.
- Determine the model of the game.
- Specify the objective of the game.
- List the rules of the game.
- Specify the roles of the players.
- Give the time frame.
- Provide all needed resources and materials.
- Pilot test the game before using it with students.

Conclude the activity by saying, "Incorporating games can be as easy as using an existing crossword puzzle on the subject you are teaching. Particularly for common board games, you can use the same board and substitute your own questions. While you and your students can create games from scratch, the emphasis should be on the process of playing and learning rather than on the look of the game itself."

Sample skill activities: Begin this section by saying, "Let's see how games can be used in interesting ways throughout the curriculum. You have already completed one game activity. Now we're going to do a couple of activities that you might want to try in your classroom. As we work through these exercises, I want you to reflect on these questions:
- What did you learn about games-adaptable information?
- How did the activity facilitate learning?
- How can games be used in each discipline?

Feel free to make comments after each activity, or wait until this portion of the workshop is completed."

Authors*: This activity shows how card games can be used to categorize information. Ahead of time, copy one set of Authors* cards for each table. Have groups at each table play the game according to generic Authors or rummy rules.

Sequences: This activity shows how games can be used to teach sequencing skills. Ahead of time, photocopy five to 10 magazine covers portraying important events, but cover the dates so they don't appear on the copies. Create one set per table, mixing their order. Each group sequences the covers chronologically.

Get on board*: This activity demonstrates how board games can be adapted to teach or review facts. Ahead of time, copy the Get on Board! rules and board* for each table. Cut index cards in half. On both halves of each card, write the title of a book. On one of the halves, write the book elements with their corresponding numbers as listed in the rules. Mix the cards with the titles only and alphabetize the others so you can have an answer file. Make one set for each table and have the groups play the game.

Processing: Divide the teachers into three groups and assign one of the sample game activities to each, asking each group to reflect on their assigned activity and answer the questions posed at the start of the session. Each group reports its conclusions.

Break: Announce that this time might be well spent examining book displays and game shelves, since the next activity will be to construct a resource list of useful games-adaptable titles.

Resources: Hand out a sample bibliography of games-adaptable sources for potential use in the classroom. Logical choices are encyclopedias, almanacs, and other fact books. Suggest ways to use them in the classroom.

As a large group, create a longer list of titles. Alternatively, teachers may want to divide into small groups by subject area to develop curriculum-specific bibliographies. In either case, use the standard brainstorm process:
- Elicit responses from individuals in turn.
- Record each title for all to see.
- Allow comments only for clarification; no judgments.
- Ask for clarification as needed.

These lists may be typed and distributed as a follow-up handout.

Lesson planning: Using an item from the Idea Starters* handout and the Teacher-Librarian Lesson Planning Process* handout from Section 5, walk the group through the teacher-librarian planning process.

Application: Divide the group into thirds and have them use the Teacher-Librarian Lesson Planning Process* handout to plan a lesson. At this time, distribute the Idea Starters* handout or give each teacher a games-adaptable source to use as a starting point. The groups may want to brainstorm a number of activities, but they should plan one activity in detail. Give them 20 minutes to summarize and record their plan and discuss the process they followed. They will then report to the large group. The resulting records may be typed up and distributed as a follow-up handout.

Wrap-up: Summarize insights that the group gained from incorporating games into the curriculum. Provide a direction for pursuing library-related activities using games. Each teacher should walk away with at least one usable idea.

Be sure the group is given at least five minutes to evaluate the workshop. This helps in planning future workshops.

In closing, thank all the facilitators and participants.

Resources	Annotated bibliographies of games-adaptable sources held by the library.
Evaluation	Each small group shares one lesson plan incorporating games. Their ideas may be typed up for follow-up distribution. By the end of the quarter teachers will share, in a departmental or faculty meeting, one lesson they taught that incorporated games. The librarian may write up the best librarian-teacher-produced lesson plans for school publications.
Variations	• Focus on one type of game: board, cards, word. • Focus on one subject area. • Modify sample classroom activities to match other levels of curriculum.

Categories

Directions: Fill in each square with a word that fits the category and starts with the letter at the top of the column. One example is done for you.

CATEGORY	L	E	A	R	N
Food	*lettuce*				
Sport					
Place					
Person					

Authors Game Cards

Virginia Hamilton	Lois Lowry	William Sleator
In the Beginning M. C. Higgins the Great House of Dies Drear Sweet Whispers, Brother Rush	*A Summer to Die* Number the Stars The Giver Find a Stranger, Say Goodbye	*House of Stairs* Interstellar Pig Others See Us Boy Who Reversed Himself
Cynthia Voigt *Izzy, Willy-Nilly* Solitary Blue Runner Dicey's Song	**Richard Peck** *Father Figure* Princess Ashley Close Enough to Touch Remembering the Good Times	**Gary Paulsen** *Dogsong* Monument Voyage of the Frog Hatchet
Walter Dean Myers *Hoops* Fallen Angels Scorpions Young Landlords	Laurence Yep *Dragonwings* Child of the Owl Rainbow People Monster Makers, Inc.	Norma Fox Mazer *Up in Seth's Room* After the Rain Downtown Dear Bill, Remember Me?

Get on Board!

START				DRAW AGAIN		
	LOSE 1 TURN					GO 2 SPACES
			DRAW AGAIN		GO 2 SPACES	
						DRAW AGAIN
FINISH!		LOSE 1 TURN				GO 2 SPACES	

Get on Board! Rules

Objective: To reach the end first.

How To Play: Players take turns tossing a die, then drawing a title card. Players then attempt to name the element of the book corresponding to the number on the die.

1 = author

2 = setting

3 = time

4 = main character

5 = climax

6 = ending

If the player identifies the element correctly, he advances on the board the same number as on the die.

Idea Starters

Ten Student Projects:

Create a scavenger hunt with answers found in books or computers.

Create a snakes and ladders game using game rules.

Create a concentration game on American symbols.

Play Twenty Questions about authors.

Create a crossword puzzle on art terms.

Do charades about historical events.

Create a Bingo game on nature.

Simulate a baseball game for math equations.

Create an observation game on maps.

Have a relay race on first aid procedures.

Notes

Expanding the Story Hour Experience

Intended audience	Elementary teachers across the curriculum.

Objectives

Teachers will
- List ways that enrichment activities can promote reading.
- Identify techniques that enrich the reading experience.
- Incorporate enrichment activities into their curriculum.

Set-up

Arrange teachers in small groups by grade level for guided practice. Display useful resources on the tables for teacher browsing. Use a large newsprint pad on an easel or an overhead projector to present ideas. Each group should have newsprint to "publish" its lesson plan and writing materials to make notes.

Workshop overview

165 minutes

Introduction:	Welcome, housekeeping details, directions	10
Rationale:	Whole language approach to reading. Why use enrichment activities?	15
Sample activities:	Story quilt*	10
	Coming to a story hour near you	15
	Story pathways*	15
	Group processing	10
Break:		10
Resources:	Bibliography and group titles	15
Lesson planning:	Model teacher-librarian planning	10
Application:	Small groups plan lesson and report out	40
Wrap-up:	Summary, evaluation, follow-up	15

Content

Early bird activity: Hand out "Extra! Extra!"* sheet. Have reading enrichment resources on tables for teachers to browse.

Introduction: Post the agenda and state the goals clearly so teachers will know what to expect. Emphasize resource-based learning and teacher-librarian collaboration.

Rationale for skill: In small groups arranged across subject area, have teachers discuss how they conduct story time and how students deal with reading. Have each group report one insight they gained about teaching strategy. Record their insights.

Discuss the whole-language approach to reading. Point out that whole language is based in contextual meaning and expression so that students bring personal meaning to reading. State the use of reading enrichment activities in the curriculum: "Reading enrichment activities encourage and reinforce enjoyment and understanding of other people's ideas. As students make a passage their own, linking minds, they grow in their knowledge of the world and they advance their expression of that experience."

Sample skill activities: Begin this section by saying, "Let's see how reading enrichment activities can be used in interesting ways throughout the curriculum. You have already experienced one reading enrichment activity. Now we're going to do a couple of activities that you might want to try in your classroom. As we work through these exercises, I want you to reflect on these questions:

• What did you learn about reading?
• How did the activity facilitate learning?
• How can reading enrichment activities be used in each discipline?

Feel free to make comments after each activity, or wait until this portion of the workshop is completed."

Story quilt*: This activity shows one way to teach and synthesize story elements. Distribute the Story Quilt* to pairs of teachers. Have them choose a story and complete the quilt squares with the appropriate information. When they are finished, have each pair share their story quilts with another pair. Suggest ways to modify the activity for youngsters. For instance, have them each draw one quilt square.

Coming to a story hour near you: This activity demonstrates how to summarize a story dramatically. Have pairs create 10-second "commercials" for stories. This is a good activity to share with the large group immediately by asking volunteers to deliver their "commercials." (A simulated TV set or radio announcer's stand adds color.)

Story pathways: This activity demonstrates how to build upon a reading interest. Model this activity by distributing the Johnny Appleseed Story Pathway*. Orally walk through the pathway with the large group. Then have groups of four develop their own pathways for other legends.

Processing: Divide the teachers into three groups and assign one of the sample skill activities to each. Have each group reflect on their assigned activity by answering the questions posed at the start of the session. Have each group report their conclusions.

Break: Announce that this time might be well spent examining book displays and shelves, since the next activity will be to construct a resource list of useful reading enrichment titles.

Resources: Hand out a sample bibliography of reading enrichment sources for potential use in the classroom. Show some lesser known titles and suggest ways to use them in the classroom.

As a large group, create a longer list of titles. Alternatively, teachers may want to divide into small groups by subject area to develop curriculum-specific bibliographies. In either case, use the standard brainstorm process:
• Elicit responses from individuals in turn.
• Record each title for all to see.
• Allow comments only for clarification; no judgments.
• Ask for clarification of titles as needed.

These lists may be typed and distributed as a follow-up handout.

Lesson planning: Using an item from the Idea Starters* handout and the Teacher-Librarian Lesson Planning Process* handout from Section 5, walk the group through the teacher-librarian planning process.

Application: Divide the group into thirds and have them use the Teacher-Librarian Lesson Planning Process* handout to plan a lesson. At this time, distribute the Idea Starters* handout or give each teacher a good reading enrichment source as a starting point. The groups may want to brainstorm a number of activities, but they should plan one activity in detail. Give them 20 minutes to summarize and record their plan and discuss the process they followed. They will then report to the large group. The resulting records may be typed up and distributed as a follow-up handout.

Wrap-up: Summarize insights that the group gained from incorporating reading enrichment into the curriculum. Provide a direction for pursuing library-related activities using reading enrichment sources. Each teacher should walk away with at least one usable idea.

Be sure the group is given at least five minutes to evaluate the workshop. This helps in planning future workshops.

In closing, thank all the facilitators and participants.

Resources   Annotated bibliographies of reading enrichment sources held by the library. Other useful resources include

Hall, Susan, *Using Picture Storybooks To Teach Literary Devices.* Phoenix: Oryx, 1990; Vol. 2, 1994.

Laughlin, Mildred, and Letty S. Watt, *Developing Learning Skills Through Children's Literature.* Phoenix: Oryx, 1986.

Watt, Letty S., and Terri Parker Street, *Developing Learning Skills Through Children's Literature, Vol. 2.* Phoenix: Oryx, 1994.

Evaluation

Each small group shares one lesson plan incorporating reading enrichment activities. Their ideas may be typed up for follow-up distribution. By the end of the quarter teachers will share in a grade-level or all-faculty meeting one lesson they taught that incorporated reading enrichment activities. The librarian may write up the best librarian-teacher-produced lesson plans for school publications.

Variations

- Focus on one type of reading enrichment activity: kinesthetic, artistic, verbal.
- Focus on one subject area.
- Modify sample classroom activities to match other levels of curriculum.

Additional information

The whole-language approach to reading has spawned hundreds of reading-related activities. Teachers should examine these guides critically because many are disguised questions-and-answer work sheets or rote learning projects. Any enrichment activity should foster creativity and critical thinking.

Extra! Extra! Read All About It!

Directions: Identify the children's story suggested by the following newspaper headlines.

Toothy Trespasser Captured Red-Handed!

Family Interrupts Housebreaker in Bed!

I Was a Kept Woman for Midgets—and Loved it!

Huff Rebuffed! Porky Proves Prowess!

Crystal Shoe Reveals Heels!

Monster Demands Death or Daughter!

Whittler Carves New Life!

Dirty Rat Cleans Out Town of Kids!

Adoptive Family Rejects Disfigured Youth!

Ivory Tower Beauty Lets It All Hang Out!

Story Quilt

POINT OF VIEW	BEGINNING	SETTING
CLIMAX	TITLE	ONE CHARACTER
TITLE	MOOD	END

Johnny Appleseed Story Pathway

Read the "Johnny Appleseed" legend

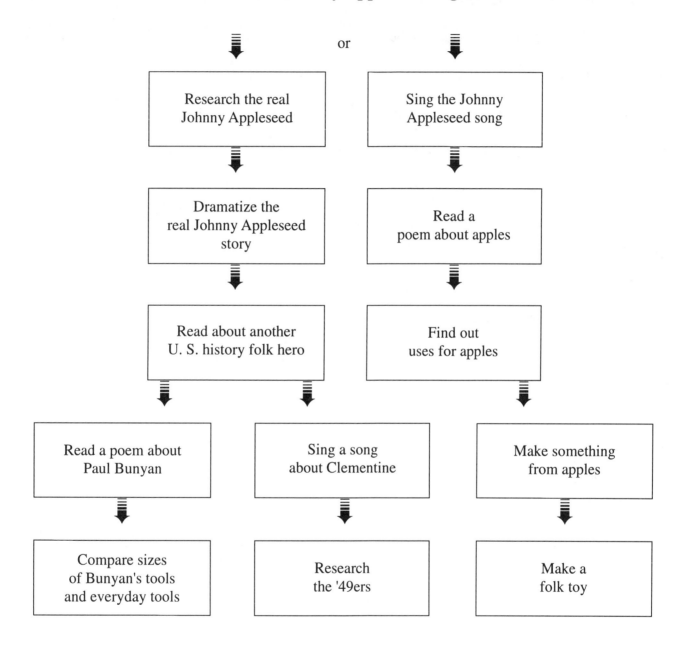

or

Research the real
Johnny Appleseed

Sing the Johnny
Appleseed song

Dramatize the
real Johnny Appleseed
story

Read a
poem about apples

Read about another
U. S. history folk hero

Find out
uses for apples

Read a poem about
Paul Bunyan

Sing a song
about Clementine

Make something
from apples

Compare sizes
of Bunyan's tools
and everyday tools

Research
the '49ers

Make a
folk toy

Idea Starters

Ten Student Projects:

Act out a story, such as *Caps for Sale.*

Draw scenes from the story and sequence them.

Make character puppets.

Dress up as story characters.

Make collages from magazine pictures related to the story.

Find a song or poem that relates to the story.

Imagine two characters from different stories meeting. Create a conversation between them.

Compare elements between two stories: setting, outcome, time span.

Create a model or diorama of a story's setting.

Create a comic strip version of a story.

The Magic of Poetry

Intended audience   Elementary teachers across the curriculum.

Objectives   Teachers will
• List ways that poetry can enrich their curriculum.
• Identify poetry resources that relate to their curriculum.
• Incorporate poetry into their curriculum.

Set-up   If the workshop is held in the library, teachers can consult the library catalog and browse the shelves for interesting poetry. Be sure to give teachers the opportunity to borrow titles that interest them. Arrange teachers in a tight semi-circle, using movable chairs. Display titles for teacher browsing. Use a large newsprint pad on an easel or an overhead projector to present information.

After break, rearrange the group by grade level or subject into smaller working groups of three to six people. Each group should have newsprint to "publish" its lesson plan and writing materials to make notes.

Reminder: Collect the poems to read ahead of time, mark them, and have them in order ready to read when the workshop begins.

Workshop overview

175 minutes

Introduction:	Welcome, housekeeping details, directions	10
Rationale:	Responding to poetry. Why use poetry?	20
Sample activities:	Poetry as movement	15
	Poetry as theme	15
	Poetry as perspective	15
	Group processing	10
Break:		10
Resources:	Bibliography and group titles	15
Lesson planning:	Model teacher-librarian planning	10
Application:	Small groups plan lesson and report out	40
Wrap-up:	Summary, evaluation, follow-up	15

Content   *Early bird activity:* Hand each person a Poetry Survey*. Display poetry resources on tables for teachers to browse.

Introduction: Post the agenda and state the goals clearly so teachers will know what to expect. Emphasize resource-based learning and teacher-librarian collaboration.

Rationale for skill: Set the tone by reading a poem. Two good choices are "Keep a Poem in Your Pocket" by Beatrice Schenk de Regniers and Eleanor Fargeon's "What Is Poetry?" If time permits, show a video from the "Good Conversations" series by Tim Podell Productions.

Begin by saying, "Everyone has a feeling about poetry. Some remember it fondly. Some write poetry as a release. Some remember memorizing it—with a sigh either of nostalgia or regret. Some love rhyme and hate free verse. Some want to sing to poetry. And some think it's just for children. Regardless, poetry is evocative."

Have people talk for a couple of minutes with their neighbors about their personal feelings about poetry, using the Poetry Survey* as a conversation starter. Afterwards, ask for some brief comments. Then have groups of four discuss how students respond to poetry. Again, draw out some group responses. Next, have the large group brainstorm the kinds of learning to be found in poetry. Record and summarize their insights. Typical responses include
• Listening skills,
• Kinesthetic learning (rhythm, movement),
• Writing skills,
• Aesthetic appreciation,
• Word play and other word skills,
• Literary conventions,
• Creativity, and
• Content information.

State the case for using poetry in the curriculum: "Poetry has the power to elevate everyday words, thoughts, and feelings. It crystallizes real experiences, stretches the imagination, and encourages personal response, for it transcends form to speak directly to the heart. I hope that one outcome for today is that you will find one poem that speaks personally to you and one poem that can be used in your class."

Sample skill activities: Begin this section by saying, "Let's see how poetry can be used in interesting ways throughout the curriculum. You have already experienced one poetry-related activity. Now we're going to do a couple of activities that you might want to try in your classroom. As we work through these exercises, I want you to reflect on these questions:
• What did you learn about poetry?
• How did the activity facilitate learning?
• How can poetry be used in each discipline?

Feel free to make comments after each activity, or wait until this portion of the workshop is completed."

Poetry as movement: This activity focuses on the sound and rhythm of poetry. First, have the group listen to the movement of poetry itself.

Encourage them to close their eyes in order to focus on their hearing sense. Good poems to read in this exercise are "Sound of Water" by Mary O'Neill, "Slowly" by James Reeves, "Silver" by Walter de la Mare, "From a Railway Carriage" by Robert Louis Stevenson, and selections from *Joyful Noise* by Paul Fleischman. A good anthology is *Rhythm Road*, edited by Ruth Gordon.

Next, have the group respond to the rhythm of poetry by moving their own bodies: clapping, finger-waving, head-bopping. Milne, Rossetti, Blake, and Longfellow are standard rhythmic poets. With teachers of young children, lead poetry finger-plays of nursery rhymes.

Poetry as theme: This activity demonstrates how poetry can be linked to curricular themes. A simple and effective way to look at U. S. history is through its poetry and songs. Lead with a poem such as Benet's "Nancy Hanks," and have the group brainstorm historical poems and songs. The anthology *From Sea to Shining Sea* exemplifies this theme. Then lead a group discussion about the insights that these poems offer.

Poetry as perspective: This activity shows the critical thinking involved in interpreting the deeper meaning of poetry. Start this activity by saying, "Poetry can turn perspectives upside-down. It gives us a chance to see the mundane in a new way. As you listen to these poems, consider these questions:
• What is the 'normal' view, and how does the poem's perspective differ?
• How do you react to the change in perspective?
• How would students respond to these poems?
• How could these poems be used in class?"

Write the questions for the group to see. Good poems to use include "Father William" by Lewis Carroll, "Adventures of Isabel" by Ogden Nash, "Disobedience" by A. A. Milne, and "Mother to Son" by Langston Hughes. After reading the poems, lead a group discussion on the guiding questions, or have small groups discuss them.

Processing: Divide the teachers into three groups and assign one of the sample skill activities to each. Have each group reflect on their assigned activity by answering the questions posed at the start of the session. Have each group report their conclusions.

Break: Announce that this time might be well spent examining book displays and poetry shelves, since the next activity will be to construct a resource list of useful poetry titles.

Resources: Hand out a sample bibliography of poetry sources for potential use in the classroom. Emphasize thematic poetry anthologies, such as sports and humor. Point out significant poetry anthologists such as Paul Janeczko, Lee Bennett Hopkins, and Myra Cohn Livingston. Show some lesser known sources that might otherwise be overlooked, such as songs and jump-rope rhymes, and suggest ways to use them in the classroom.

As a large group, create a longer list of titles. Alternatively, teachers may want to divide into small groups by subject area to develop curriculum-specific bibliographies. In either case, use the standard brainstorm process:
- Elicit responses from individuals in turn.
- Record each title for all to see.
- Allow comments only for clarification; no judgments.
- Ask for clarification as needed.

These lists may be typed and distributed as a follow-up handout.

Lesson planning: Using an item from the Idea Starters* handout and the Teacher-Librarian Lesson Planning Process* handout from Section 5, walk the group through the teacher-librarian planning process.

Application: Divide the group into thirds and have them use the Teacher-Librarian Lesson Planning Process* handout to plan a lesson. At this time, distribute the Idea Starters* handout or give each teacher a poetry source as a starting point. The groups may want to brainstorm a number of activities, but they should plan one activity in detail. Give them 20 minutes to summarize and record their plan and discuss the process they followed. They will then report to the large group. The resulting records may be typed up and distributed as a follow-up handout.

Wrap-up: Summarize insights that the group gained from incorporating poetry into the curriculum. Provide a direction for pursuing library-related activities using poetry. Each teacher should walk away with at least one usable idea.

Be sure the group is given at least five minutes to evaluate the workshop. This helps in planning future workshops.

In closing, thank all the facilitators and participants.

Resources   Annotated bibliographies of poetry sources held by the library. Other useful resources include

Chatton, Barbara, *Using Poetry Across the Curriculum*. Phoenix: Oryx, 1993.

Smith, Richard J., *Using Poetry To Teach Reading and Language Arts*. Metuchen NJ: Scarecrow, 1984.

Evaluation   Each small group shares one lesson plan incorporating poetry. Their ideas may be typed up for follow-up distribution. By the end of the quarter teachers will share in a department or all-faculty meeting one lesson they taught that incorporated poetry. The librarian may write up the best librarian-teacher-produced lesson plans for school publications.

Variations
- Focus on one type of poetry: humor, rhyme, ballads.
- Focus on one subject area or theme.
- Modify sample classroom activities to match other levels of curriculum.

Additional information
Music, art, and movement classes can plan cooperative poetry sessions with grade-level teachers.

Poetry Survey

Directions: Complete the following phrases.

1. Poetry is _____
   _____
   _____
   _____

2. As a child I remember poetry _____
   _____
   _____
   _____

3. Writing poetry is _____
   _____
   _____
   _____

4. Poetry makes me _____
   _____
   _____
   _____

5. My favorite poem _____
   _____
   _____
   _____

6. Poetry should _____
   _____
   _____
   _____

7. The last time I heard poetry _____
   _____
   _____
   _____

8. Poetry in school _____
   _____
   _____
   _____

9. I just want to say _____
   _____
   _____

Idea Starters

Ten Student Projects:

Dance to poetry.

Make a song out of a poem.

Do choral reading.

Finger-paint to poetry.

Collect poems by theme, author, or just "likes."

Write a poem in the style of a poet.

Illustrate poems.

Act out a poem.

Have puppets recite poetry.

Have a poetry festival.

Notes

Looking with the Inner Eye: Appreciating Illustration

Intended audience   Elementary teachers across the curriculum.

Objectives   Teachers will
- List ways that illustrations can enrich their curriculum.
- Identify illustration resources that relate to their curriculum.
- Incorporate illustrations into their curriculum.

Set-up   Arrange teachers in small groups heterogeneously for the first guided practice. Rearrange them by grade level after break. Display illustration resources on the tables for teacher browsing. Use a large newsprint pad on an easel or an overhead projector to present information. Each group should have newsprint to "publish" its lesson plan and writing materials to make notes.

Workshop overview   170 minutes

Introduction:	Welcome, housekeeping details, directions	10
Rationale:	Contributions to the field of illustration. Why use illustrations?	15
Sample activities:	Illustration as technique	15
	Illustration as art	15
	Illustration as story	15
	Group processing	10
Break:		10
Resources:	Bibliography and group titles	15
Lesson planning:	Model teacher-librarian planning	10
Application:	Small groups plan lesson and report out	40
Wrap-up:	Summary, evaluation, follow-up	15

Content   *Early bird activity:* Hand out Illustrations Bingo* cards. Have illustration resources on tables for teachers to browse.

Introduction: If the workshop is held in the library, teachers can consult the library catalog and browse the shelves for interesting books. Be sure to give teachers the opportunity to borrow interesting titles. Post the agenda and state the goals clearly so teachers will know what to expect. Emphasize resource-based learning and teacher-librarian collaboration.

If possible, introduce the workshop by viewing Weston Wood's sound filmstrip "How a Picture Book is Made" or video "The Lively Art of Picture Books," if those resources are available.

Begin by following up on the early bird activity, saying, "The bingo sheet of illustration elements points out the variety of approaches that you and your students can use to appreciate illustrations. Feel free to jot down relevant titles throughout the day. You can even shout 'Bingo!' At the end of the day, we'll see how full our illustration bingo will become." You can offer bingo prizes if you wish, such as an illustrated bookmark.

Start the formal session by drawing upon personal experiences. Share some of your favorite picture book illustrations, perhaps from your own childhood, telling what about them "touched" you. Have each person share their favorites with another person. Ask for a few responses from the group as a whole. Summarize by saying, "Illustrations are a powerful medium, for they touch us emotionally as well as aesthetically. As we look at the elements that make illustrations so truly telling, we can help our students respond to them personally and creatively."

Rationale for skill: In small groups, arranged across subject area and grade, have teachers brainstorm a list of insights that can be drawn from illustrations. Have them discuss how students respond to illustrations. Have each group report one insight about students and illustrations. Record their findings.

Show a couple of sample books, both picture and nonfiction titles. You may focus entirely on picture books or include older nonfiction sources. State the case for using illustrations in the curriculum: "Illustrations provide information and insights that transcend verbal language. Whether they are cross-sections or microscopic photography, illustrations can show us worlds we would ordinarily not see. Illustrations are artistic statements, to be appreciated for their technique and composition. Illustrations also tell stories, complementing or replacing text to enrich our imaginations. Finally, illustrations speak directly to our hearts and show us beauty even in sadness."

Sample skill activities: Begin this section by saying, "Let's see how illustrations can be used in interesting ways throughout the curriculum. You have already done one illustrations-related activity. Now we're going to do a couple of activities that you might want to try in your classroom. As we work through these exercises, I want you to reflect on these questions:
• What artistic elements are found in the illustrations?
• What artistic techniques are found in the illustrations?
• What literary or informational elements do the illustrations provide?
• How did the activity facilitate learning?
• How can illustrations be used for each class?

Feel free to make comments after each activity, or wait until this portion of the workshop is completed."

Illustration as technique: This activity focuses on the impact of technique on the quality of illustrations. Using the Illustrations Bingo* sheet as a starting point, lead a group brainstorming session to list different techniques that artists use. Typical responses include drawing, painting, collage, print making, photography, sewing, and computer art. Encourage more detailed examples of the above techniques. Using the illustrated books already on the tables, have the teachers, in pairs, determine which techniques are used in the book and how that illustrator's particular approach contributes to the story or information. Model the activity by taking one book, such as Eric Carle's *The Very Hungry Caterpillar*, and verbally describing his techniques. To extend the activity, have pairs share their findings with another pair.

Illustration as art: This activity details the artistic elements common to all illustrations. Start by reviewing basic artistic elements: line, color, light and dark, shape, space, and composition. Show an example of each and list the elements for the group to see. Another option is to model the activity by critically examining the artistic elements of one book, such as Paul Goble's *The Girl Who Loved Wild Horses*. A list of books exemplifying each element is included in the Illustration as Art Bibliography*. Have pairs examine the same book they used in the first activity from this perspective. To extend the activity, have them compare their findings with another book.

Illustration as story: This activity demonstrates how illustrations provide story material. Start by reviewing and listing elements of storytelling: point of view, mood, pacing, sense of place and people, plot, theme, and style. Point out that illustrations can enrich and reinforce the textual story. Mention how not only the pictures themselves but their placement on the pages can help make the story a real page-turner (a prime example being Jim Stevenson's *Quick, Turn the Page*). If needed, model the activity by pointing out the use of illustration as story element using David Wiesner's *Tuesday*. Have pairs analyze this book or others in terms of the illustrations' contribution to the story. Extend the activity by having them analyze another book in the same way and compare the two.

Processing: Divide the teachers into three groups and assign one of the sample skill activities to each. Have each group reflect on their assigned activity by answering the questions posed at the start of the session. Have each group report their conclusions.

Break: Announce that this time might be well spent examining book displays and shelves, since the next activity will be to construct a resource list of useful illustration titles.

Resources: Hand out a sample bibliography of illustration sources for potential use in the classroom. Include some lesser known titles that might otherwise be overlooked. Emphasize the fact that older students can use picture books successfully because they are analyzing them visually rather than verbally.

As a large group, create a longer list of titles. Alternatively, teachers may want to divide into small groups by subject area to develop curriculum-specific bibliographies. In either case, use the standard brainstorm process:

- Elicit responses from individuals in turn.
- Record each title for all to see.
- Allow comments only for clarification; no judgments.
- Ask for clarification as needed.

These lists may be typed and distributed as a follow-up handout.

Lesson planning: Using an item from the Idea Starters* handout and the Teacher-Librarian Lesson Planning Process* handout from Section 5, walk the group through the teacher-librarian planning process.

Application: Divide the group into thirds and have them use the Teacher-Librarian Lesson Planning Process* handout to plan a lesson. At this time, distribute the Idea Starters* handout or give each teacher an illustration source as a starting point. The groups may want to brainstorm a number of activities, but they should plan one activity in detail. Give them 20 minutes to summarize and record their plan and discuss the process they followed. They will then report to the large group. The resulting records may be typed up and distributed as a follow-up handout.

Wrap-up: Summarize insights that the group gained from incorporating illustration into the curriculum. Provide a direction for pursuing library-related activities using illustrations. Each teacher should walk away with at least one usable idea.

Be sure the group is given at least five minutes to evaluate the workshop. This helps in planning future workshops.

In closing, thank all the facilitators and participants.

Resources   Annotated bibliographies of illustration sources held by the library. Other useful resources include

Marantz, Sylvia, *Picture Books for Looking and Learning*. Phoenix: Oryx, 1992.

Evaluation   Each small group shares one lesson plan incorporating illustrations. Their ideas may be typed up for follow-up distribution. By the end of the quarter teachers will share in a grade-level or all-faculty meeting one lesson they taught that incorporated illustrations. The librarian may write up the best librarian-teacher-produced lesson plans for school publications.

Variations

- Focus on one type of illustration: by technique or by artistic element.
- Focus on one subject area: wordless books, nonfiction, art.
- Modify sample classroom activities to match other levels of curriculum.

Additional information

Illustrations can be used for art courses as well as for content-based classes. Illustrations should also be considered in light of cultural features.

Illustrations Bingo

Directions: Complete the bingo card by locating and listing one book that contains the element listed in each category. Titles may not be used more than once.

Hidden pictures	Black & white line drawings	Collage	Folk art	About animals
Cross-sections	Native American motif	Wordless	Stitchery technique	Holiday
Paper cutouts	Watercolor	FREE!	Photographs	Latino motif
Book YOU read as a child	Fairy or folk tale	Border art	Asian motif	Optical illusions
African motif	Mother Goose	Historical	Humorous	Uses primary colors

Illustration as Art Bibliography

Line
Gag, Wanda, *Millions of Cats*
Grahame, Kenneth, *The Wind in the Willows*
Macauley, David, *Pyramid*
McCloskey, Robert, *The Story of Ferdinand*
Williams, Garth, *Little House on the Prairie*

Color
Brown, Margaret Wise, *Goodnight Moon*
Burkert, Nancy, *The Nightingale*
Emberley, Barbara, *Drummer Hoff*
Martin, Bill, *Brown Bear, Brown Bear, What Do You See?*
Remkiewicz, Frank, *The Last Time I Saw Harris*

Light and Dark
Fisher, Leonard Everett, *The Death of the Evening Star*
Minarik, Else, *Little Bear's Visit*
Rylant, Cynthia, *When I Was Young in the Mountains*
Sendak, Maurice, *Outside Over There*
Van Allsberg, Chris, *The Mysteries of Harris Burdick*

Shape
Brown, Marcia, *Once a Mouse*
Keats, Erza Jack, *The Snowy Day*
McDermott, Gerald, *Arrow to the Sun*
Ungerer, Tomi, *The Three Robbers*
Lionni, Leo, *Frederick*

Space
Anno, Mitsumasa, *Anno's U.S.A.*
Burton, Virginia Lee, *The Little House*
Goble, Paul, *The Girl Who Loved Wild Horses*
Mosel, Arlene, *The Funny Little Woman*
Weisner, David, *Free Fall*

Composition
Aardema, Verna, *Who's in Rabbit's House?*
Barrett, Judy, *Cloudy with a Chance of Meatballs*
Brett, Jan, *The Mitten*
Kuskin, Karla, *Roar and More*
Wood, Audrey, *The Napping Book*

A good source is Lyn Ellen Lacy's *Art and Design in Children's Picture Books*. ALA, 1986.

Idea Starters

Ten Student Projects:

Study how a picture book is made.

Create a piece of artwork in the same style as an illustration.

Compare two illustrations in terms of artistic elements or techniques.

Look at illustrations in terms of emotions: which seem happy, serious, mysterious, silly?

Evaluate illustrations in terms of the culture they represent.

Paint a picture using the same color palette as the artist.

Look at illustrations in terms of geometric shapes.

Compare two books about the same period in history or the same setting.

Compare two artists' treatment of the same story, such as a fairy tale.

Study a variety of illustrations by the same artist.

Arithmetic Through Reading

Intended audience   Elementary teachers across the curriculum.

Objectives   Teachers will
- List ways that reading can enrich their curriculum.
- Identify books that relate to their curriculum.
- Incorporate reading into their curriculum.

Set-up   Arrange teachers in small groups by subject area for guided practice. Display interesting fiction and fact books on the tables for teacher browsing. Use a large newsprint pad on an easel or an overhead projector to present information. Each group should have newsprint to "publish" its lesson plan and writing materials to make notes.

Workshop overview   160 minutes

Introduction:	Welcome, housekeeping details, directions	10
Rationale:	Reading and arithmetic: Why use reading sources?	15
Sample activities:	The look of numbers*	10
	The myth of mathematics	10
	Decoding mathematics*	15
	Group processing	10
Break:		10
Resources:	Bibliography and group titles	15
Lesson planning:	Model teacher-librarian planning	10
Application:	Small groups plan lesson and report out	40
Wrap-up:	Summary, evaluation, follow-up	15

Content   *Early bird activity:* Hand out the Proverbial Mathematics* activity sheet. Have resources on display for teachers to browse. Titles may be laid out on the tables.

Introduction: Post the agenda and state the goals clearly so teachers will know what to expect. Emphasize resource-based learning and teacher-librarian collaboration.

Distribute answer sheet* for Proverbial Mathematics activity. State that while this activity is geared to adults, it can be modified for young learners by asking them to answer with the numbers that go with the phrase; for example, "There were how many blind mice?"

If time permits (approximately 15 more minutes), introduce the workshop by sharing the book (or film) *The Dot and the Line* by Norman Juster.

Formalize the introduction by saying, "Usually mathematics is associated with numbers and problem-solving. Yet creative writers have successfully woven mathematical concepts into fictional works. By experiencing mathematics through literature, students develop an aesthetic appreciation for mathematics as a mind set."

Rationale for skill: To clarify the workshop's intent, lead a large group discussion on mathematical concepts in literature by asking open-ended questions such as

- What picture books or nursery rhymes use numbers or shapes?
- How do folktales and fairy tales makes use of numbers?
- What are some examples of riddles or jokes involving mathematical concepts? (For instance, "How do you divide 13 apples among 19 people?" "Make applesauce.")
- What science fiction or fantasy writing depict mathematical ideas?

Alternatively, have small groups arranged across grade levels take one of the questions above and brainstorm ideas, sharing their insights with the larger group.

Have the large group brainstorm a list of mathematical concepts that might arise in literature. Typical answers include logic, measurement, topology, consumer math, and probability.

Summarize the case for teaching arithmetic through reading within the curriculum by saying, "Neither mathematics nor literature exists in a vacuum. By combining these two areas, you can help students respond imaginatively to their worlds. In addition, students can intuit surprisingly complex mathematical concepts, such as topology, when experiencing them in picture book form."

Sample skill activities: Begin this section by saying, "Let's see how literature can be used in interesting ways with mathematics. You have already done one mathematics-related activity. Now we're going to do a couple of activities that you might want to try in your classroom. As we work through these exercises, I want you to reflect on these questions:

- What mathematical concepts are introduced?
- How do the mathematical concepts aid the story? What would happen if they were omitted?
- How can literature and mathematics be combined?

Feel free to make comments after each activity, or wait until this portion of the workshop is completed."

The look of numbers*: Provide pairs with books from the list provided to analyze in terms of their mathematical concepts. Have the pairs share their findings with their table mates. While typical concept books on counting and shapes may be included, provide more literary books with subtler treatments.

An alternative to literary works are books that show numbers in different cultures and different times. Good places to start are Leonard Fisher's *Number Art* and *Calendar Art*, Muriel Feelings' *Menjo Means One*, and Jim Haskin's series on *Count Your Way Through . . . .* Books on the history of writing and mathematics often have sections on other mathematical symbols such as hieroglyphics and cuneiform.

Still another approach (expanded in the resource section) is eclectic. Distribute a variety of books to analyze—literary, visual, magic, code, mysteries, puzzles, riddles, recreational.

The myth of mathematics: This activity demonstrates how numbers and other mathematical concepts have literary connotations. Have one pair per table brainstorm numerical connotations, such as "Seven is a lucky number" and "You can have three wishes." Have the other pair brainstorm stories or rhymes that contain a number, such as "Three Little Kittens" and *Snow White and the Seven Dwarfs*. Have the pairs share their lists.

Decoding mathematics*: This activity shows a way to transform letters into numbers. Distribute the Decoding Mathematics* activity, or substitute samples from your own collection, giving Version A to one pair at each table and Version B to the other pair. Have them solve the code and write a sentence using the code. Have pairs share their codes. To extend the activity, have pairs exchange code sheets or create their own codes.

Processing: Divide the teachers into three groups and assign one of the sample skill activities to each. Have each group reflect on their assigned activity by answering the questions posed at the start of the session. Have each group report their conclusions.

Break: Suggest that this time might be well spent examining book displays and shelves, since the next activity will be to construct a resource list of useful titles.

Resources: Begin this activity by saying, "By now you can see that mathematics exists throughout the curriculum, and reading offers insights about many aspects of mathematics." Hand out a sample bibliography of sources for potential use in the classroom. Include some lesser known titles that might otherwise be overlooked. Potential areas include magic, puzzles and riddles, string figures, origami, history, calligraphy, optical illusions, biology (geometry in nature), poetry, mysteries, and books of records or firsts.

As a large group, create a longer list of titles. Alternatively, teachers may want to divide into small groups by subject area to develop curriculum-specific bibliographies. In either case, use the standard brainstorm process:

- Elicit responses from individuals in turn.
- Record each title for all to see.
- Allow comments only for clarification; no judgments.
- Ask for clarification as needed.

These lists may be typed and distributed as a follow-up handout.

Lesson planning: Using an item from the Idea Starters* handout and the Teacher-Librarian Lesson Planning Process* handout from Section 5, walk the group through the teacher-librarian planning process.

Application: Divide the group into thirds and have them use the Teacher-Librarian Lesson Planning Process* handout to plan a lesson. At this time, distribute the Idea Starters* handout or give each teacher a math reading source as a starting point. The groups may want to brainstorm a number of activities, but they should plan one activity in detail. Give them 20 minutes to summarize and record their plan and discuss the process they followed. They will then report to the large group. The resulting records may be typed up and distributed as a follow-up handout.

Wrap-up: Summarize insights that the group gained from combining reading and mathematics. Provide a direction for pursuing library-related activities using these sources. Each teacher should walk away with at least one usable idea.

Be sure the group is given at least five minutes to evaluate the workshop. This helps in planning future workshops.

In closing, thank all the facilitators and participants.

Resources
Annotated bibliographies of library holdings that combine reading and mathematics. Other useful resources include

Braddon, Kathryn L., Nancy J. Hall, and Dale Taylor, *Math Through Children's Literature*. Englewood CO: Libraries Unlimited, 1993.

Evaluation
Each small group shares one lesson plan incorporating reading and mathematics. Their ideas may be typed up for follow-up distribution. By the end of the quarter teachers will share in a grade-level or all-faculty meeting one lesson they taught that incorporated reading and math. The librarian may write up the best librarian-teacher-produced lesson plans for school publications.

Variations
- Focus on one type of source: literary, recreational, informational.
- Focus on one subject area.
- Customize the workshop by grade level. Modify sample classroom activities to match specific grade level curriculum.
- Focus on one mathematical concept: numbers, shapes, size, problem-solving.

Additional information

This workshop can be modified to blend reading, particularly literary works, with other subjects such as science or art.

Proverbial Mathematics

Directions: Each equation contains the initials of words that will make it correct. To solve, supply the missing words. For example, 7 = D. in a W. would be 7 = Days in a Week.

1. 2000 = P. in a T.

2. 1001 = A. N.

3. 52 = C. in a D.

4. 13 = S. on the A. F.

5. 3 = B. M.

6. 40 = T. with A. B.

7. 24 = B. B. in a P.

8. 64 = S. on a C.

9. 7 = D. with S. W.

10. 1000 = W. that a P. is W.

Answers to Proverbial Mathematics

1.   2000 = Pounds in a Ton

2.   1001 = Arabian Nights

3.   52 = Cards in a Deck

4.   13 = Stripes on the American Flag

5.   3 = Blind Mice

6.   40 = Thieves with Ali Baba

7.   24 = Blackbirds Baked in a Pie

8.   64 = Squares on a Checker/Chessboard

9.   7 = Dwarfs with Snow White

10.   1000 = Words that a Picture is Worth

The Look of Numbers: A Beginning List

Agee, Jon, *The Incredible Painting of Felix Clousseau*
Anno, Mitsumasa, *Anno's Hat Trick*
Black, Quentin, *Improbable Records*
Brown, Marcie, *Once a Mouse*
Budney, Blossom, *A Kiss is Round*
Crosswell, Volney, *How to Hide a Hippopotamus*
Gag, Wanda, *Millions of Cats*
Geisel, Theodore, *Yertle the Turtle*
Ginsburg, Mirra, *Two Greedy Bears*
Hulme, Joy, *Sea Squares*
Hutchens, Pat, *The Doorbell Rang*
Lionni, Leo, *Inch by Inch*
Lobel, Arnold, *Frog and Toad Are Friends*
MacDonald, George, *The Light Princess*
Mahy, Margaret, *The Seven Chinese Brothers*
Milhous, Katherine, *Turnip*
Numeroff, Laura, *If You Give a Mouse a Cookie*
Silverstein, Shel, *The Missing Piece*
Thurber, James, *Many Moons*
Thurber, James, *Thirteen Clocks*
Toban, Tana, *Look! Look! Look!*
Zemach, Margot, *It Could Always Be Worse*

Sources:
National Council of Teachers of Mathematics, *Mathematics Library:
Elementary and Junior High School*
Nichols, Danita, "Math Concept Books: What We Have, What We Need,"
School Library Journal (Dec., 1993) p. 41-42
Spann, Mary Beth, "Linking Literature and Math," *Instructor* (April, 1992) p. 54

Decoding Mathematics

Version A:

Directions: Using the code key, decode the following phrase:

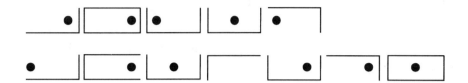

Each letter is represented by a dot set within the grid.

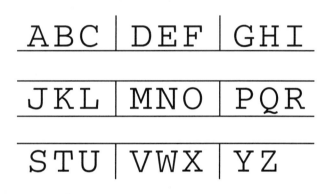

Thus, A = •⌋ and W = ⌈ • ⌋

Decoding Mathematics

Version B:

Directions: Using the code key, decode the following phrase:

XXIII VIII V XIV   IX XIV   XVIII XV XIII V

Each letter is represented by its corresponding Roman numeral, 1 through 26.
Thus, A = I and Z = XXVI.

Idea Starters

Ten Student Projects:

Use or create a code.

Use or create a visual number system.

Read or create a poem that incorporates a mathematical concept.

Create a collage that illustrates a mathematical concept.

Create a mathematics word problem based on a story.

Compare two visual number systems.

Read or create riddles, jokes, or puzzles that incorporate mathematical concepts.

Act out a story that incorporates a mathematical concept.

Read or create a picture book that incorporates a mathematical concept.

Read or create a fable that illustrates a mathematical concept.

<u>Notes</u>

Beyond Book Reports

Intended audience   Middle school teachers across the curriculum.

Objectives   Teachers will
- List alternatives to book reports that can enrich their curriculum.
- Incorporate alternatives to book reports into their curriculum.

Set-up   Arrange teachers in small groups by subject area for guided practice. Display resources on the tables for teacher browsing. Use a large newsprint pad on an easel or an overhead projector to present information. Each group should have newsprint to "publish" its lesson plan and writing materials to make notes.

Workshop overview

170 minutes		
Introduction:	Welcome, housekeeping details, directions	10
Rationale:	Why use alternatives to book reports?	15
Sample activities:	Prologue, sequel	15
	Character voice	15
	Story leader	15
	Group processing	10
Break:		10
Resources:	Bibliography and group titles	15
Lesson planning:	Model teacher-librarian planning	10
Application:	Small groups plan lesson and report out	40
Wrap-up:	Summary, evaluation, follow-up	15

Content

Early bird activity: Have early birds list alternatives to book reports on newsprint pad. Or distribute the Book Reading Survey* and use that as a discussion starter among pairs.

Introduction: Post the agenda and state the goals clearly so teachers will know what to expect. Emphasize resource-based learning and teacher-librarian collaboration.

Rationale for skill: Lead a large-group brainstorming session to list alternatives to book reports, using the early bird newsprint lists as a starting point. Have the group discuss how these alternatives would be beneficial. Record their findings.

Show a couple of sample alternatives to book reports. State the case for assigning alternatives to book reports: "Since students react to books in different ways and learn in different modes, it follows that we should look for ways to assess their reading other than book reports. Today we will be exploring other means of synthesizing and sharing books and their meanings."

Sample skill activities: Begin this section by saying, "Let's see how alternatives to book reports can be used in interesting ways throughout the curriculum. You have already listed and talked about some alternatives. Now we're going to do a couple of activities that you might want to try in your classroom. As we work through these exercises, I want you to reflect on these questions:

- What did you learn about alternatives to book reports?
- How did the activity facilitate learning?
- How can alternatives to book reports be used in each discipline?

Feel free to make comments after each activity, or wait until this portion of the workshop is completed."

Prologue, sequel: This activity emphasizes the time frame of a book and encourages students to extrapolate a story line before and beyond the plot. Have pairs choose a story such as *Wind in the Willows* or *Huckleberry Finn* and imagine a prologue or sequel to the story. If time permits, they may share their creations with another pair.

Character voice: This activity encourages exploration of a character's point of view. Have pairs write a letter in the voice of a chosen character or create a monologue in a character's voice. If time permits, have pairs make up dialogues in their characters' voices.

Story leader: This activity focuses on a story's dramatic elements. Have pairs choose a story and storyboard a movie leader to a film version of the story.

Processing: Divide the teachers into three groups and assign one of the sample skill activities to each. Have each group reflect on their assigned activity by answering the questions posed at the start of the session. Have each group report their conclusions.

Break: Suggest that this time might be well spent examining book displays and shelves, since the next activity will be to construct a resource list of useful titles.

Resources: Hand out a sample bibliography of sources for potential use in the classroom. Include some lesser known titles that might otherwise be overlooked.

As a large group, create a longer list of titles. Alternatively, teachers may want to divide into small groups by subject area to develop curriculum-specific bibliographies. In either case, use the standard brainstorm process:

- Elicit responses from individuals in turn.
- Record each title for all to see.
- Allow comments only for clarification; no judgments.
- Ask for clarification as needed.

These lists may be typed and distributed as a follow-up handout.

Lesson planning: Using an item from the Idea Starters* handout and the Teacher-Librarian Lesson Planning Process* handout from Section 5, walk the group through the teacher-librarian planning process.

Application: Divide the group into thirds and have them use the Teacher-Librarian Lesson Planning Process* handout to plan a lesson. At this time, distribute the Idea Starters* handout or give each teacher a good alternative to a book report as a starting point. The groups may want to brainstorm a number of activities, but they should plan one activity in detail. Give them 20 minutes to summarize and record their plan and discuss the process they followed. They will then report to the large group. The resulting records may be typed up and distributed as a follow-up handout.

Wrap-up: Summarize insights that the group gained about using alternatives to book reports. Provide a direction for pursuing library-related activities using alternatives to book reports. Each teacher should walk away with at least one usable idea.

Be sure the group is given at least five minutes to evaluate the workshop. This helps in planning future workshops.

In closing, thank all the facilitators and participants.

Resources	Annotated bibliographies of alternatives to book reports held by the library.
Evaluation	Each small group shares one lesson plan incorporating alternatives to book reports. Their ideas may be typed up for follow-up distribution. By the end of the quarter teachers will share in a departmental or all-faculty meeting one lesson they taught that incorporated alternatives to book reports. The librarian may write up the best librarian-teacher-produced lesson plans for school publications.
Variations	• Focus on one type of alternative: dramatizations, multimedia presentations, charts. • Focus on one subject area. • Modify sample classroom activities to match other levels of curriculum.
Additional information	Particularly with the emphasis on portfolio assessments and project-based learning, alternatives to book reports are an educational necessity—besides being more engaging for students.

Book Reading Survey

Directions: Complete the following sentences.

1. I like a book that _____

_____

2. When I enjoy a book, I share it by _____

_____

3. I think the most important part of a book is _____

_____

4. The purpose of book reports is _____

_____

5. The way I can tell that a student has read a book is _____

_____

6. I think TV or movie versions of books are _____

_____

7. The way I decide to read a book is _____

_____

8. The best way to encourage reading is _____

_____

9. Another way to assess reading would be _____

_____

10. The most important thing about reading is _____

_____

Idea Starters

Ten Student Projects:

Make a collage of the book's elements.

Create a comic strip version of the book.

Advertise the book.

Create a time line of the book.

Create a crossword puzzle for the book.

Create a board game based on the book.

Dramatize the book.

Make a model of the book's setting.

Compare two books' characters.

Compare books written by the same author, especially in a series.

Notes

Myth and Legend Across the Curriculum

Intended audience Middle school teachers across the curriculum.

Objectives Teachers will
- List ways that myths and legends can enrich their curriculum.
- Identify myths and legends that relate to their curriculum.
- Incorporate myths and legends into their curriculum.

Set-up Arrange teachers in small groups by subject area for guided practice. Display myth and legend books on the tables for teacher browsing. Use a large newsprint pad on an easel or an overhead projector to present information. Each group should have newsprint to "publish" its lesson plan and writing materials to make notes.

Workshop overview 165 minutes

Introduction:	Welcome, housekeeping details, directions	10
Rationale:	Why use myths and legends?	15
Sample activities:	Character study	10
	Modern-day myths	15
	Social values of myths and legends	15
	Group processing	10
Break:		10
Resources:	Bibliography and group titles	15
Lesson planning:	Model teacher-librarian planning	10
Application:	Small groups plan lesson and report out	40
Wrap-up:	Summary, evaluation, follow-up	15

Content *Early bird activity:* Hand out Sayings from Myths* activity sheet. Have myth and legend resources displayed on tables for teachers to browse.

Introduction: Post the agenda and state the goals clearly so teachers will know what to expect. Emphasize resource-based learning and teacher-librarian collaboration.

Rationale for skill: In small groups, arranged across subject areas, have teachers brainstorm nuggets of wisdom to be found in myths and legends. Have them discuss how students deal with myths and legends. Have each group report on one insight about student use. Record the insights they share.

Use a standard dictionary or Funk and Wagnalls' *Standard Dictionary of Folklore, Mythology, and Legend* to define "myth" and "legend." State the case for using myths and legends in the curriculum: "Myths and legends provide a literary and folkloric way to look at social norms and values. They help students find their own solutions to social problems and inner conflicts in a detached, yet emotional, way. Myths and legends also mirror cultural perspectives and demonstrate relative concepts of good and evil, right and wrong."

Sample skill activities: Begin this section by saying, "Let's see how myths and legends can be used in interesting ways throughout the curriculum. You have already engaged in one myth-and-legend-related activity. Now we're going to do a couple of activities that you might want to try in your classroom. As we work through these exercises, I want you to reflect on these questions:
• What did you learn about mythical and legendary information?
• How did the activity facilitate learning?
• How can myths and legends be incorporated in each discipline?

Feel free to make comments after each activity, or wait until this portion of the workshop is completed."

Character study: This activity demonstrates how myths and legends can be used to look at character traits and values. Have pairs choose a legendary figure, such as Paul Bunyan or Achilles, and examine that hero in terms of his or her personal qualities. Guiding questions might be written out:
• How old is the character?
• What does the character look like?
• What distinguishing marks or habits does he or she have?
• How does the character speak and act?
• Who are the character's friends and enemies?

If time permits, have pairs share their character analyses with another pair, or have them act out their character.

Modern-day myths: This activity shows how myths can be transformed. Have pairs choose a myth and place it in a modern setting. Cite Leonard Bernstein's treatment of the *Romeo and Juliet* story in *West Side Story* as an example. If time permits, have pairs share their "modern-day myths" with another pair.

Social values of myths and legends: This activity encourages critical thinking in terms of values. Have pairs choose a myth or legend and examine it critically in terms of social norms and values. If time permits, have pairs share their analyses with another pair.

Processing: Divide the teachers into three groups and assign one of the sample skill activities to each. Have each group reflect on their assigned activity by answering the questions posed at the start of the session. Have each group report their conclusions.

Break: Suggest that this time might be well spent examining book displays and shelves, since the next activity will be to construct a resource list of useful myth and legend titles.

Resources: Hand out a sample bibliography of myths and legends for potential use in the classroom. Include some lesser known titles that might otherwise be overlooked and suggest ways to use them in the classroom.

As a large group, create a longer list of titles. Alternatively, teachers may want to divide into small groups by subject area to develop curriculum-specific bibliographies. In either case, use the standard brainstorm process:
• Elicit responses from individuals in turn.
• Record each title for all to see.
• Allow comments only for clarification; no judgments.
• Ask for clarification as needed.

These lists may be typed and distributed as a follow-up handout.

Lesson planning: Using an item from the Idea Starters* handout and the Teacher-Librarian Lesson Planning Process* handout from Section 5, walk the group through the teacher-librarian planning process.

Application: Divide the group into thirds and have them use the Teacher-Librarian Lesson Planning Process* handout to plan a lesson. At this time, distribute the Idea Starters* handout or give each teacher a myth or legend to use as a starting point. The groups may want to brainstorm a number of activities, but they should plan one activity in detail. Give them 20 minutes to summarize and record their plan and discuss the process they followed. They will then report to the large group. The resulting records may be typed up and distributed as a follow-up handout.

Wrap-up: Summarize insights that the group gained from incorporating myths and legends into the curriculum. Provide a direction for pursuing library-related activities using myths and legends. Each teacher should walk away with at least one usable idea.

Be sure the group is given at least five minutes to evaluate the workshop. This helps in planning future workshops.

In closing, thank all the facilitators and participants.

Resources   Annotated bibliographies of myths and legends held by the library. In addition, useful sources for studying myths and legends include

Bosma, Bette, *Fairy Tales, Fables, Legends, and Myths: Using Folk Literature in Your Classroom.* Metuchen NJ: Scarecrow, 1992.

Evaluation

Each small group shares one lesson plan incorporating myths and legends. Their ideas may be typed up for follow-up distribution. By the end of the quarter teachers will share in a departmental or all-faculty meeting one lesson they taught that incorporated myths and legends. The librarian may write up the best librarian-teacher-produced lesson plans for school publications.

Variations

- Focus on one type of myth or legend: by culture, motif, or style.
- Focus on one subject area.
- Modify sample classroom activities to match other levels of curriculum.

Additional information

An interesting discussion topic might be to explore the fine distinctions among "myth," "legend," "fairy tale," and "folktale."

Sayings From Myths

Directions: Identify the myth or legend associated with the following phrases:

1. Beware of Greeks bearing gifts
2. Bearing the weight of the world on one's shoulders
3. See the handwriting on the wall
4. Pillar of salt
5. Honi soit qui mal y pense
6. Ides of March
7. Peeping Tom
8. Robbing the rich to give to the poor
9. All he touches turns to gold
10. My kingdom for a horse

Answers:
1. Trojan horse
2. Atlas
3. Balthazar
4. Lot's wife
5. Knights of the Garter
6. Julius Caesar's death
7. Lady Godiva
8. Robin Hood
9. King Midas
10. Richard III

Brainstorm words and phrases that come directly from mythology.
Example: Achilles' heel

Idea Starters

Ten Student Projects:

Act out a myth or legend.

Relate myths and legends to social and psychological issues such as sibling rivalry or parental control.

Connect myths and legends to countries or cultures.

Compare two different treatments of the same or similar myth.

Find a poem about a myth or legend.

Research the historical context of a myth or legend.

Construct a family tree for mythical figures.

Explore modern urban legends.

Dress up as a mythological or legendary character.

Mapping the World

Intended audience   Middle school teachers across the curriculum.

Objectives   Teachers will
- Identify a variety of atlases and maps that relate to their curriculum.
- Interpret atlas information in light of their curriculum.
- Design lessons incorporating atlas information.

Set-up   Ideally, the room should be arranged with separate tables to facilitate small group work. A wide variety of atlases should be available, a sampling of them displayed on each table. Newsprint pads, markers, and note-taking supplies should also be placed at each table. The facilitator should have an overhead projector and screen to project transparencies of maps and workshop notes.

Workshop overview   160 minutes

Introduction:	Welcome, housekeeping details, directions	10
Rationale:	Background notes on atlases. Why use atlases?	15
Sample activities:	Same place, different information	10
	Forecast forum	15
	Graphic information	10
	Group processing	10
Break:		10
Resources:	Bibliography and group titles	15
Lesson planning:	Model teacher-librarian planning	10
Application:	Small groups plan lesson and report out	40
Wrap-up:	Summary, evaluation, follow-up	15

Content   *Early bird activity:* Display atlases for teachers to examine. Give early birds an Atlas Puzzle* to complete.

Introduction: Seat teachers in groups of four around tables. Post the agenda and state the goals clearly so teachers will know what to expect. Emphasize resource-based learning and teacher-librarian collaboration.

Rationale for skill: Have teachers brainstorm as many types of atlases as possible, writing down their ideas. Have them share their lists in pairs. Have those pairs then brainstorm the kinds of information to be found in atlases and maps, and have them share those lists with another pair. Have the groups report their findings, and add to the lists. Typical lists of atlas types might include
- Political,
- Physical,
- Historical,

- Various sized geographic areas (neighborhood to universe), and
- Thematic (environmental, ethnic).

Typical lists of atlas and map information could include
- Statistical,
- Relative standings,
- Measurement,
- Descriptive (vegetation, climate),
- Events (battles, discoveries),
- Biographical,
- Verbal (descriptive, literary), and
- Visual (illustrations, photos).

Using the lists the groups have generated, reinforce the concept that atlases can be used across the curriculum. For example,
- Math students can develop charts and graphs.
- Science students can discover cause-and-effect relationships between land features and climate or biology.
- English students can locate literary sites.
- Art students can draw original maps.

Close this activity by saying, "Atlases and their maps are particularly exciting learning resources because they incorporate visual and graphic elements and help develop both linear and nonlinear thinking skills. They also reinforce the idea of multiple perspectives."

Sample skill activities: Begin this section by saying, "Let's see how atlases can be used in interesting ways throughout the curriculum. You have already engaged in one atlas-related activity before the workshop started. Now we're going to do a couple of activities that you might want to try in your classroom. As we work through these exercises, I want you to reflect on these questions:
- What information do these sources contain?
- How did the activity facilitate learning?
- How can atlases be used in each discipline?

Feel free to make comments after each activity, or wait until this portion of the workshop is completed."

Same place, different information: This activity shows how each atlas presents information differently. Facilitate this activity by placing two atlases covering overlapping geographic areas on each table ahead of time. Have each pair choose an atlas; then have each group of four choose a common geographic area. The pairs of teachers list as many kinds of information for their area as they can find in their atlas. The pairs then compare their lists.

Forecast forum: This activity shows the use of data analysis. Rotate atlases among tables. Each pair examines two maps within an atlas to discover a pattern or correlation. For example, one map might show elevation and another show vegetation for the same area; the type of vegetation relates to the elevation. Another example might be looking at a population density map and a poverty map and trying to find a correlation between those two conditions.

Each pair then predicts what the trend will be, based on the prior pattern, for another map or region. In the first example, on the basis of elevation a pair might predict the type of vegetation for a different geographic area. To extend the activity, have each pair share their correlation with another pair, and have that other pair extrapolate the information for a different map.

Graphic information: This activity demonstrates how to transfer data from one form to another. Each pair sets up the grid for a chart based on information culled from a map. For example, a number of countries could be listed across the top of a graph with the five largest cities ranked by population in the vertical column. Extend the activity by having pairs trade atlases and generate a second grid for the same map.

Processing: Divide the teachers into three groups and assign one of the sample skill activities to each. Have each group reflect on their assigned activity by answering the questions posed at the start of the session. Have each group report their conclusions.

Break: Suggest that this time might be well spent examining book displays and atlas shelves, since the next activity will be to construct a resource list of useful atlas titles.

Resources: Hand out a sample bibliography of atlases for potential use in the classroom. As a large group, have the teachers share the titles they found useful. Emphasize the fact that maps can be found in other sources besides atlases, such as encyclopedias and travel books. This point is critical for libraries with limited collections. Show some lesser known titles that might otherwise be overlooked and suggest ways to use them in the classroom. Good sources to include are *National Geographic Historical Atlas of the United States*, *Cultural Atlas of Japan*, *Atlas of Animal Migration*, and *Atlas of Fantasy*.

As a large group, create a longer list of titles. Alternatively, teachers may want to divide into small groups by subject area to develop curriculum-specific bibliographies. In either case, use the standard brainstorm process:
• Elicit responses from individuals in turn.
• Record each title for all to see.
• Allow comments only for clarification; no judgments.
• Ask for clarification as needed.

These lists may be typed and distributed as a follow-up handout.

Lesson planning: Using an item from the Idea Starters* handout and the Teacher-Librarian Lesson Planning Process* handout from Section 5, walk the group through the teacher-librarian planning process.

Application: Divide the group into thirds and have them use the Teacher-Librarian Lesson Planning Process* handout to plan a lesson. At this time, distribute the Idea Starters* handout or give each teacher an atlas to use as a starting point. The groups may want to brainstorm a number of activities, but they should plan one activity in detail. Give them 20 minutes to summarize and record their plan and discuss the process they followed. They will then report to the large group. The resulting records may be typed up and distributed as a follow-up handout.

Wrap-up: Summarize insights that the participants gained from incorporating atlases into the curriculum. Provide a direction for pursuing library-related activities using atlases. Each teacher should walk away with at least one usable idea.

Be sure the group is given at least five minutes to evaluate the workshop. This helps in planning future workshops.

In closing, thank all the facilitators and participants.

Resources	Annotated bibliographies of atlases held by the library.
Evaluation	Each small group shares one lesson plan incorporating atlases. Their ideas may be typed up for follow-up distribution. By the end of the quarter teachers will share in a departmental or all-faculty meeting one lesson they taught that incorporated atlases. The librarian may write up the best librarian-teacher-produced lesson plans for school publications.
Variations	• Focus on one type of atlas: by feature, topic, or area. • Focus on one subject area. Customize the workshop for each department. • Modify sample classroom activities to match other levels of curriculum.
Additional information	Map-reading and map-production skills can be generalized to other visual literacy competencies.

Atlas Puzzle

Directions: Identify each outlined state.

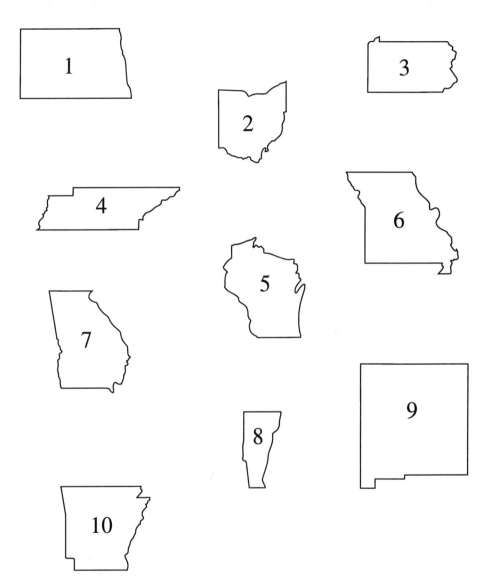

Idea Starters

Ten Student Projects:

Create transparencies of geographic areas over time, and make inferences about the differences.

Create original maps and legends to explain symbols.

Compare explorer maps of the same geographic areas.

Compare different map projections.

Use maps to locate famous people, such as scientists or musicians. Make inferences based on population distribution.

Transform a two-dimensional map into a three-dimensional one.

Based on maps that use percentages, create different kinds of charts to visualize the same information.

Compare two general atlases for the same area. Then compare a general and a specialized atlas for the same area.

Compare maps in two different languages.

Using map information, reconstruct a historic trip. Take into account geography, climate, road conditions.

Creating and Using Databases

Intended audience	High school teachers across the curriculum.
Objectives	Teachers will

- List ways that databases can enrich their curriculum.
- Identify database resources that relate to their curriculum.
- Develop a database.
- Incorporate database techniques into their curriculum.

Set-up   If the workshop is held in the library, teachers can consult the library catalog and browse the shelves for interesting database resources. Be sure to give teachers the opportunity to borrow interesting titles. Arrange teachers in pairs for each computer. Use overheads and computer projection panels to present information. Make sure that computers operate and have the needed software. A good choice is *Works*. A ready-made database should be created for teachers to test; a natural choice would be a school inventory of software or videotapes.

Workshop overview   180 minutes

Introduction:	Welcome, housekeeping details, directions	10
Rationale:	Why use databases?	15
Sample activities:	Using a database	20
	Creating a database	40
	Group processing	10
Break:		10
Resources:	Bibliography and group titles	15
Lesson planning:	Model teacher-librarian planning	10
Application:	Small groups plan lesson and report out	35
Wrap-up:	Summary, evaluation, follow-up	15

Content   *Early bird activity:* Have participants begin to experiment with an existing in-house database. Display database resources on tables for teachers to browse.

Introduction: Post the agenda and state the goals clearly so teachers will know what to expect. Emphasize resource-based learning and teacher-librarian collaboration.

Rationale for skill: Define "database" as a collection of data organized for easy retrieval and arrangement. Point out that a library collection constitutes a database. Lead a large-group brainstorming session on other examples of databases. Note that databases need not be computerized, but for the sake of this workshop print-based data will be transferred into computer format for easier manipulation.

State the case for incorporating databases in the curriculum by saying, "Particularly when data are limited but used in a variety of ways, databases are useful ways of organizing and analyzing information. User-developed databases blend information skills and content knowledge as students learn to collect data for study, determine which information is important, and organize and access information. In decision-making, they learn to test hypotheses and explore possible correlations among data."

Sample skill activities: Begin this section by saying, "Let's see how databases can be used in interesting ways throughout the curriculum. We are going to do a couple of activities that you might want to try in your classroom. As we work through these exercises, I want you to reflect on these questions:
- What did you learn about databases?
- How did the activity facilitate learning?
- How can databases be used in each discipline?

Feel free to make comments after each activity, or wait until this portion of the workshop is completed."

Using a database: This activity shows how to manipulate existing databases in different ways. Using an existing database, such as Tom Snyder's database software series or an in-house database, guide pairs in their use. The basic steps should be as follows:
- Start the session and open the desktop.
- Open the application and locate the database file.
- Walk through the fields to understand the kind of information included.
- Sort the database according to a field, with a possible secondary sort. As an instructional tool, the database should be considered the raw data for testing a hypothesis. For example, for a database of the U. S. Presidents, the following hypothesis could be made: "Presidents are becoming younger." The first sort would be age when elected. A secondary sort would be date of first election. By rearranging data the user can test the hypothesis easily.
- Optionally, save the report in a file or print it.

Creating a database: This activity demonstrates the steps in creating a computer database. To make the best use of databases requires careful designing of the database template: that is, the fields and their sequence. Point out some factors to consider when designing a database format:
- What is the purpose of the information and database? Think of all the possible ways to manipulate the information.
- What kind of information will be included?
- What will be the field names and labels?
- What field is the most important? Put it first.
- Are similar types of fields grouped together?
- Is the sequence of fields logical?

Post these questions for the group to see or make a handout of the factors.

To facilitate this activity, distribute a photocopy of a simple collection of data, such as a chart from a statistical almanac. Walk the group through the process of defining fields and making records. (For the sake of time, limit the number of records to 10.) Then have each pair develop a hypothesis based on the data, and test the hypothesis by sorting the created database.

Processing: Have several pairs report on their process. Have the group reflect on the activities by answering the questions posed at the start of the session.

Break: Suggest that this time might be well spent examining book displays and shelves, since the next activity will be to construct a resource list of useful database-related titles.

Resources: Hand out a sample bibliography of database sources for potential use in the classroom. Show some lesser known titles that might otherwise be overlooked and suggest ways to use them in the classroom.

As a large group, create a longer list of titles. Alternatively, teachers may want to divide into small groups by subject area to develop curriculum-specific bibliographies. In either case, use the standard brainstorm process:
• Elicit responses from individuals in turn.
• Record each title for all to see.
• Allow comments only for clarification; no judgments.
• Ask for clarification as needed.

These lists may be typed and distributed as a follow-up handout.

Lesson planning: Using an item from the Idea Starters* handout and the Teacher-Librarian Lesson Planning Process* handout from Section 5, walk the group through the teacher-librarian planning process.

Application: Divide the group into thirds and have them use the Teacher-Librarian Lesson Planning Process* handout to plan a lesson. At this time, distribute the Idea Starters* handout or give each teacher a database source to use as a starting point. The groups may want to brainstorm a number of activities, but they should plan one activity in detail. Give them 20 minutes to summarize and record their plan and discuss the process they followed. They will then report to the large group. The resulting records may be typed up and distributed as a follow-up handout.

Wrap-up: Summarize insights that the participants gained from incorporating databases into the curriculum. Provide a direction for pursuing library-related activities using databases. Each teacher should walk away with at least one usable idea.

Be sure the group is given at least five minutes to evaluate the workshop. This helps in planning future workshops.

In closing, thank all the facilitators and participants.

Resources   Annotated bibliographies of database sources held by the library.

Evaluation   Each small group shares one lesson plan incorporating databases. Their ideas may be typed up for follow-up distribution. By the end of the quarter teachers will share in a departmental or all-faculty meeting one lesson they taught that incorporated databases. The librarian may write up the best librarian-teacher-produced lesson plans for school publications.

Variations
- Focus on one type of database: demographics, rankings, opinion.
- Focus on one subject area.
- Modify sample classroom activities for younger grade levels.
- Focus on database report formats: charts, spreadsheets, graphs.

Additional information   Encourage the use of CD-ROM databases; some generate their own graphs.

Idea Starters

Ten Student Projects:

Survey the school and create a database of the findings.

Develop a database of volunteer job opportunities.

Develop a student "yellow pages."

Develop a speakers' list database.

Develop a database of personal records.

Develop databases that can be used by other students.

Develop book review databases.

Develop databases about people.

Develop databases about countries.

Develop databases about courses.

Notes

The Research Process

Intended audience   High school teachers across the curriculum.

Objectives   Teachers will
• Understand the research process.
• Work with the librarian to design research units.

Set-up   If the workshop is held in the library, teachers can consult the library catalog and browse the shelves. Give teachers the opportunity to borrow interesting titles. Arrange teachers in small groups by subject area for guided practice. Use newsprint pads on easels and overhead transparencies to present information. Each group should have newsprint to "publish" its lesson plan and writing materials to make notes.

Workshop overview

	150 minutes	
Introduction:	Welcome, housekeeping details, directions	10
Rationale:	What is the research process? Why partner with librarians?	15
Sample activities:	The research process	40
	Group processing	10
Break:		10
Lesson planning:	Model teacher-librarian planning	10
Application:	Small groups plan lesson and report out	40
Wrap-up:	Summary, evaluation, follow-up	15

Content   *Early bird activity:* Hand out the Teacher-Librarian Partner Check Sheet*. Display research resources on tables for teachers to browse.

Introduction: Post the agenda and state the goals clearly so teachers will know what to expect. Emphasize resource-based learning and teacher-librarian collaboration.

Rationale for skill: In small groups arranged across subject area have teachers brainstorm how they presently conduct research projects. Have them discuss how they work with the librarian during the process. Have each group report on one insight about teacher-librarian partnerships. Record their insights.

State the case for cooperative planning for research projects across the curriculum by saying, "Research projects require a close partnership between the classroom teacher and the librarian. The librarian brings a knowledge of resources and information skills. The classroom teacher brings a knowledge of content area and of the students. It takes time to coordinate activities, but it results in more meaningful and interactive student learning."

Sample skill activities: Begin this section by saying, "Let's see how research can be used in interesting ways throughout the curriculum. You have already started thinking about research process planning. Now we're going to do a couple of activities that you might want to try in your classroom. As we work through these exercises, I want you to reflect on these questions:
- What did you learn about research?
- How did the activity facilitate learning?
- How can research be used in each discipline?

Feel free to make comments after each activity, or wait until this portion of the workshop is completed."

The research process: This activity shows the steps for successful research units. Distribute the Research Planning Process* checklist. Walk the group through the process, providing time frames and tips for maximizing the use of the library and staff. To make the experience more concrete, use a sample research project to illustrate the steps.

Processing: Have the group reflect on the activity by answering the questions posed at the start of the session. Report their reflections.

Break: Suggest that this time might be well spent examining book displays and shelves, since the next activity will be to construct a lesson plan.

Lesson planning: Walk the group through the Teacher-Librarian Lesson Planning Process* handout from Section 5.

Application: Divide the group into thirds and have them use the Teacher-Librarian Lesson Planning Process* handout to plan a lesson. They may want to brainstorm a number of activities, but they should plan one activity in detail. Give them 20 minutes to summarize and record their plan and discuss the process they followed. They will then report to the large group. The resulting records may be typed up and distributed as a follow-up handout.

Wrap-up: Summarize insights that the participants gained from incorporating research into the curriculum. Provide a direction for pursuing library-related activities for research projects. Each teacher should walk away with at least one usable idea.

Be sure the group is given at least five minutes to evaluate the workshop. This helps in planning future workshops.

In closing, thank all the facilitators and participants.

Resources   Annotated bibliographies of research sources held by the library.

Evaluation   Each small group shares one lesson plan incorporating research. Their ideas may be typed up for follow-up distribution. By the end of the quarter teachers will share in a departmental or all-faculty meeting one lesson they taught that incorporated research. The librarian may write up the best librarian-teacher-produced lesson plans for school publications.

Variations

- Focus on one type of research: pro and con, primary and secondary sources, content analysis.
- Focus on one subject area.
- Modify sample classroom activities for other levels of curriculum.

Teacher-Librarian Partner Check Sheet

Directions: Rank how often you work with the librarian to do the following tasks when planning a research project. 1 indicates never; 5 indicates always.

Task	Never	Seldom	Sometimes	Usually	Always
Define content objectives	1	2	3	4	5
Define information skills objectives	1	2	3	4	5
Define prerequisite skills	1	2	3	4	5
Define prerequisite knowledge	1	2	3	4	5
Define present knowledge base	1	2	3	4	5
Define content to present	1	2	3	4	5
Define research product	1	2	3	4	5
Know available library sources	1	2	3	4	5
Determine circulation policy	1	2	3	4	5
Know what content to present	1	2	3	4	5
Determine time frame	1	2	3	4	5
Design guided practice	1	2	3	4	5
Determine grouping	1	2	3	4	5
Individualize instruction	1	2	3	4	5
Choose evaluation method	1	2	3	4	5
Determine who will instruct	1	2	3	4	5
Determine who will evaluate	1	2	3	4	5

Research Planning Process

- Teacher-librarian interview:
  - ☐ Determine research product.
  - ☐ Determine librarian's role.
  - ☐ Evaluate available library resources.
  - ☐ Determine circulation policies.
  - ☐ Determine need for bibliography or "pathway."
- General research issues:
  - ☐ Choosing and defining a topic
  - ☐ Key words
  - ☐ Locational tools
  - ☐ Research strategies
  - ☐ Evaluating resources
  - ☐ Citing sources, plagiarism
- Student steps (*Note:* students should hand in something each session):
  - ☐ Define subject and key words.
  - ☐ Get background information.
  - ☐ Find aspects of topic.
  - ☐ Organize information.
  - ☐ Synthesize findings.
  - ☐ Draw conclusions.

Note: A beneficial activity is for students to document and share their research activity each class session. The teacher, librarian, and other students can provide suggestions for further work.

- Possible aspects for research:
  - ☐ History
  - ☐ Laws and regulations
  - ☐ Leading persons and organizations
  - ☐ Statistics and facts
  - ☐ Pros and cons
  - ☐ Future issues and trends
- Evaluation:
  - ☐ Of report or research product
  - ☐ Of research process
  - ☐ Of teaching technique and partnership

<u>Notes</u>

Exploring Careers Across the Curriculum

Intended audience   High school teachers across the curriculum.

Objectives   Teachers will
- List ways that career exploration can enrich their curriculum.
- Identify career exploration resources that relate to their curriculum.
- Incorporate career exploration into their curriculum.

Set-up   If the workshop is held in the library, teachers can consult the library catalog and browse the shelves for interesting career information. Be sure they have an opportunity to borrow interesting titles. Arrange teachers in small groups by subject area for guided practice. Display useful career exploration resources on the tables for the teachers to browse. Use a large newsprint pad on an easel or overhead transparencies to present information. Each group should be supplied with newsprint to "publish" its ideas and writing materials to take notes.

Workshop overview   175 minutes

Introduction:	Welcome, housekeeping details, directions	10
Rationale:	Why incorporate career exploration?	15
Sample activities:	Class into career	10
	People in careers	20
	Career resumes	20
	Group processing	10
Break:		10
Resources:	Bibliography and group titles	15
Lesson planning:	Model teacher-librarian planning	10
Application:	Small groups plan lesson and report out	40
Wrap-up:	Summary, evaluation, follow-up	15

Content   *Early bird activity:* Hand out copies of the Career Exploration* activity sheet. Display career exploration resources on tables for teachers to browse.

Introduction: Post the agenda and state the goals clearly so teachers will know what to expect. Emphasize resource-based learning and teacher-librarian collaboration.

Rationale for skill: In small groups arranged across subject area, have teachers discuss how they currently incorporate career information in their curriculum and how students deal with career exploration. Have each group report one insight about students and career exploration. Record their insights.

State the case for incorporating career exploration in the curriculum by saying, "One of the main goals of education is to prepare students to enter the working world and contribute to society. As students explore themselves and the curriculum, they need to see models of successful workers so they can project themselves into those roles. As teachers, we should not only teach our subjects and the context in which they operate, but also help our students prepare themselves to interact professionally in those areas. Resources on occupations and vocational and college guidance help students on a personal level to intellectually experience these possibilities."

Sample skill activities: Begin this section by saying, "Let's see how career exploration can be used in interesting ways throughout the curriculum. You have already completed one career exploration activity. Now we are going to do a couple of activities that you might want to try in your classroom. As we work through these exercises, I want you to reflect on these questions:
• What did you learn about career exploration information?
• How did the activity facilitate learning?
• How can career exploration be incorporated in each discipline?

Feel free to make comments after each activity, or wait until this portion of the workshop is completed."

Class into career: This activity transfers academic skills into the work realm. Ahead of time, photocopy representative pages from the *Occupational Outlook Handbook* or similar references. Distribute them to same-subject pairs of teachers. Have the pairs identify the skills needed in the job and relate them to course content. Then have pairs brainstorm ways to help students make the transition from course work to career work. If time permits, have pairs share their ideas with another pair.

People in careers: This activity provides role models for students with various career interests. Distribute volumes of *Current Biography* or similar references, preferably one per pair. Have pairs choose someone in their discipline and examine the person's career path and preparation. If time permits, have pairs compare two people in the same field or contrast their first choice with someone in another field.

Career resumes: This activity relates biographical information and resume writing skills. Show where subject-specific biography reference books are located in the library and have one person in each pair locate a relevant volume. Each pair reads about one person in their field and creates a resume based on the person's life. A good follow-up exercise right after break is to collect the resumes, read them aloud, and have the group guess the person's identity.

Processing: Divide the teachers into three groups and assign one of the sample skill activities to each. Have each group reflect on their assigned activity by answering the questions posed at the start of the session. Each group reports its conclusions.

Break: Suggest that this time might be well spent examining book displays and college and career exploration shelves, since the next activity will be to construct a resource list of useful career exploration titles.

Resources: Hand out a sample bibliography of college and career exploration sources for potential use in the classroom. Show some lesser known titles that might otherwise be overlooked and suggest ways to use them in the classroom. Potential areas include guides to college majors, personality and interest inventories, biographies and fictionalized biographies, computer databases, and CD-ROMs.

As a large group, create a longer list of titles. Alternatively, teachers may want to divide into small groups by subject area to develop curriculum-specific bibliographies. In either case, use the standard brainstorm process:
• Elicit responses from individuals in turn.
• Record each title for all to see.
• Allow comments only for clarification; no judgments.
• Ask for clarification as needed.

These lists may be typed and distributed as a follow-up handout.

Lesson planning: Using an item from the Idea Starters* handout and the Teacher-Librarian Lesson Planning Process* from Section 5, walk the group through the teacher-librarian planning process.

Application: Divide the group into thirds and have them use the Teacher-Librarian Lesson Planning Process* to plan a lesson. At this time, distribute the Idea Starters* handout or give each teacher a career exploration source to use as a starting point. The groups may want to brainstorm a number of activities, but they should plan one activity in detail. Give them 20 minutes to summarize and record their plan and discuss the process they followed. They will then report to the large group. The resulting records may be typed up and distributed as a follow-up handout.

Wrap-up: Summarize insights that the participants gained from incorporating career exploration into the curriculum. Provide a direction for pursuing library-related activities using career exploration sources. Each teacher should walk away with at least one usable idea.

Be sure the group is given at least five minutes to evaluate the workshop. This helps in planning future workshops.

In closing, thank all the facilitators and participants.

Resources   Annotated bibliographies of career exploration sources held by the library.

Evaluation   Each small group shares one lesson plan incorporating career exploration. Their ideas may be typed up for follow-up distribution. By the end of the quarter teachers will share in a departmental or all-faculty meeting one lesson they taught that incorporated career exploration. The librarian may write up the best librarian-teacher-produced lesson plans for school publications.

Variations

- Focus on one aspect of career exploration: college preparation, skills, demographics, the world of work.
- Focus on one subject area.
- Modify sample classroom activities for younger grade levels.

Additional information

This workshop should reflect the school's existing career program, if a college or career center is in place and staffed. If it is staffed, the workshop is most effective when team-planned and team-implemented by all those concerned with career exploration.

Career Exploration

Directions: Determine whether the following statements are true or false.

1. Between 1990 and 2005 the civilian labor force will have a net loss in numbers.

2. For the period 1990–2005 men will leave the labor force in greater numbers than women by more than four million.

3. The highest labor force growth for women will be experienced by African Americans.

4. The labor force will continue to age.

5. Today's teenage females will have a 40 percent chance of heading a family with children.

6. Labor force participation for women is highest in the 25-to-34-year-old group.

7. Men will account for 40 percent of the labor force entrants between 1990 and 2005.

8. Females earn 75 percent of what their male counterparts earn.

9. Most teenagers can expect paid employment for 25 to 45 years of their lives.

10. The greatest employment sector over the next 20 years will be in services.

Answers:
F, T, F (Asians), T, T, F (35-44%), T,F (50%), T, T

Idea Starters

Ten Student Projects:

Explore job jargon.

Create a chart that shows historical trends by tracing careers over time.

Conduct real or mock interviews with successful career people.

Create a game about careers.

Pick one major career field, such as music, and find related jobs that cross the curriculum (e.g., acoustics technician, music librarian, instrument maker).

Research job equity.

Chart industries by state or age.

Develop a "day in the life of" a career.

Research child labor laws.

Research jobs and gender trends over time.

Curriculum by the Numbers: Using Statistical Sources

Intended audience	High school teachers across the curriculum.

Objectives

Teachers will
- List ways that statistics can enrich their curriculum.
- Identify statistical resources that relate to their curriculum.
- Incorporate statistics into their curriculum.

Set-up

Group teachers by subject area for guided practice. Display statistical resources on the tables for the teachers to browse. Use a large newsprint pad on an easel or overhead transparencies to present information. Each group should be supplied with newsprint to "publish" its ideas and writing materials to take notes.

Workshop overview

160 minutes

Introduction:	Welcome, housekeeping details, directions	10
Rationale:	Contributions to the field of statistics. Why use statistics?	15
Sample activities:	Hidden numbers	10
	Rank and file	10
	How to lie with statistics	15
	Group processing	10
Break:		10
Resources:	Bibliography and group titles	15
Lesson planning:	Model teacher-librarian planning	10
Application:	Small groups plan lesson and report out	40
Wrap-up:	Summary, evaluation, follow-up	15

Content

Early bird activity: Hand out Statistics About You* sheet. Display statistical resources on tables for teachers to browse.

Introduction: Post the agenda and state the goals clearly so teachers will know what to expect. Emphasize resource-based learning and teacher-librarian collaboration.

As a warm-up, do a quick poll of the audience. Find out facts such as years of experience, degree of importance they attach to statistics (on a scale of one to 10), their degree of comfort in using statistics, and other areas of possible workshop interest. Chart the results on newsprint or transparency, and lead the group in a brief analysis of the figures.

Rationale for skill: In small groups arranged across subject area, have teachers brainstorm types of information found in statistical format. Have them discuss how students deal with statistics. Have each group report one insight about students and statistics. Record their insights.

Next, *define statistics.* One definition is "Numerical facts and data that have been collected, classified, analyzed, or interpreted." Point out that statistics can be considered within both scientific and social contexts. Show a couple of example books that contain statistics. Classic examples are almanacs and encyclopedias. *The Statistical Abstract of the United States* is another standby.

State the case for incorporating statistics in the curriculum by saying, "Statistics play a significant role in our lives. Major decisions are based on polls and other data-gathering activities. These raw data constitute good examples of primary sources that students can analyze and interpret visually, mathematically, and verbally. The issue of interpretation is particularly important, since statistics can be misused to justify one's own bias. Particularly since numerical competence is necessary in today's world, the critical use of statistical information is a skill that crosses curricular lines."

Sample skill activities: Begin this section by saying, "Let's see how statistics can be used in interesting ways throughout the curriculum. You have already completed one statistical exercise. Now we are going to do a couple of activities that you might want to try in your classroom. As we work through these exercises, I want you to reflect on these questions:
- What did you learn about statistical information?
- How did the activity facilitate learning?
- How can statistics be incorporated in each discipline?

Feel free to make comments after each activity, or wait until this portion of the workshop is completed."

Hidden numbers: This activity demonstrates how often statistics are used. Distribute a magazine to each person and ask them to find statistical information in it. (Try to give four different kinds of magazines to each table of teachers, such as sports, news, fashion, history). Have the group at each table share their findings with each other.

Rank and file: This activity shows how statistics can be analyzed in several ways. Have teachers in pairs find a statistical table and generate another table by ranking the top 10 items according to another criterion. For instance, an alphabetical list of states with their populations can be rearranged from most to least populated. Have each pair share their list with another pair.

How to lie with statistics: This activity demonstrates how statistics can be misinterpreted. Distribute the How To Lie With Statistics* work sheet. Give the participants time to read the passage and share their reactions.

Processing: Divide the teachers into three groups and assign one of the sample skill activities to each. Have each group reflect on their assigned activity by answering the questions posed at the start of the session. Each group reports its conclusions.

Break: Suggest that this time might be well spent examining book displays and shelves, since the next activity will be to construct a resource list of useful statistical titles.

Resources: Hand out a sample bibliography of statistical sources for potential use in the classroom. Show some lesser known titles that might otherwise be overlooked and suggest ways to use them in the classroom. Good sources are newspapers, government publications, online databases, student surveys, directories, sports books, and science references.

As a large group, create a longer list of titles. Alternatively, teachers may want to divide into small groups by subject area to develop curriculum-specific bibliographies. In either case, use the standard brainstorm process:
• Elicit responses from individuals in turn.
• Record each title for all to see.
• Allow comments only for clarification; no judgments.
• Ask for clarification as needed.

These lists may be typed and distributed as a follow-up handout.

Lesson planning: Using an item from the Idea Starters* handout and the Teacher-Librarian Lesson Planning Process* handout from Section 5, walk the group through the teacher-librarian planning process.

Application: Divide the group into thirds and have them use the Teacher-Librarian Lesson Planning Process* handout to plan a lesson. At this time, distribute the Idea Starters* handout or give each teacher a statistical source to use as a starting point. The groups may want to brainstorm a number of activities, but they should plan one activity in detail. Give them 20 minutes to summarize and record their plan and discuss the process they followed. They will then report to the large group. The resulting records may be typed up and distributed as a follow-up handout.

Wrap-up: Summarize insights that the participants gained from incorporating statistics into the curriculum. Provide a direction for pursuing library-related activities using statistical sources. Each teacher should walk away with at least one usable idea.

Be sure the group is given at least five minutes to evaluate the workshop. This helps in planning future workshops.

In closing, thank all the facilitators and participants.

Resources	Annotated bibliographies of statistical sources held by the library.
Evaluation	Each small group shares one lesson plan incorporating statistical sources. Their ideas may be typed up for follow-up distribution. By the end of the quarter teachers will share in a departmental or all-faculty meeting one lesson they taught that incorporated statistics. The librarian may write up the best librarian-teacher-produced lesson plans for school publications.
Variations	• Focus on one type of statistics: demographics, rankings, opinions. • Focus on one subject area. Customize the workshop for each department. • Modify sample classroom activities to match younger grade levels. • Focus on statistical measures such as standard deviation, correlations, and the like.
Additional information	Students should know how to read, interpret, *and* produce statistical information. Statistics can be used in writing and research to support claims or prove hypotheses.

Statistics About You

Directions: On the form below, jot down as much statistical information as you can about yourself, writing down both the number and the subject. Then ask two colleagues to provide you their statistics about the same subject. A couple of subjects are provided to get you started. (*Note*: People are allowed to "pass" on a statistic or to invent a number.)

Category	Name (Self):	Name:	Name:
Number of pets			
Age of car			
Age when decided to become a teacher			
Number of years teaching			

How to Lie with Statistics

Directions: Read and respond to the following excerpt. What are the implications? How can the concept be applied to your classroom?

"In the space of one hundred and seventy-six years the Lower Mississippi has shortened itself two hundred and forty-two miles. That is an average of a trifle over one mile and a third per year. Therefore, any calm person, who is not blind or idiotic, can see that in the Old Oolitic Silurian Period, just a million years ago next November, the Lower Mississippi River was upward of one million three hundred thousand miles long, and stuck out over the Gulf of Mexico like a fishing-rod. And by the same token any person can see that seven hundred and forty-two years from now the Lower Missisisippi will be only a mile and three-quarters long, and Cairo and New Orleans will have joined their streets together, and be plodding comfortably along under a single mayor and a mutual board of aldermen. There is something fascinating about science. One gets such wholesale returns of conjecture out of such a trifling investment of fact."

Mark Twain, *Life on the Mississippi*

Idea Starters

Ten Student Projects:

Make different types of graphs for the same information.

Conduct, graph, and analyze student polls.

Conduct in-depth descriptive statistical analyses on numerical data.

Take one geographic area and find a variety of statistics on it; compare findings.

Compare statistical information from different sources on the same topic.

Explore cases where statistical information is used to promote one side's opinion.

Produce a list of record statistics: highest, greatest, oldest, first.

Find statistics that influence political decisions.

Find statistics to follow a time line.

Use statistics for comparisons of playing fields, animal sizes, or energy consumption.

Notes

Encouraging your Child to Read

Intended audience   Parents of children in elementary grades.

Objectives   Parents will
- List ways that they can help their children enjoy reading.
- Identify book selection tools.

Set-up   Arrange parents in small groups by child's grade level for guided practice. Display resources on the tables for parents to browse. Use a large newsprint pad on an easel or overhead transparencies to present information. Each group should be supplied with newsprint to "publish" its ideas and writing materials to take notes.

Workshop overview   145 minutes

Introduction:	Welcome, housekeeping details, directions	10
Rationale:	Why involve parents?	15
Sample activities:	Selecting books	15
	Reading with your child	15
	Group processing	10
Break:		10
Resources:	Bibliography	15
Activity planning:	Small groups plan reading activities and report out	40
Wrap-up:	Summary, evaluation, follow-up	15

Content   *Early bird activity:* Hand out Reading Encouragement Checklist*. Display resources on tables for parents to browse.

Introduction: Post the agenda and state the goals clearly so parents will know what to expect. Emphasize resource-based learning and parent-librarian collaboration.

Rationale for skill: Have parents in pairs review the Reading Encouragement Checklist*. Have each pair report one insight about their children's reading. Record their insights.

Point out that parents are the single most important factor in a child's reading habits and that children establish their reading patterns in the elementary school years. Even illiterate parents can share picture books with their children. They can listen to their children read. They can share stories with their children. (If most parents in the workshop are illiterate, share the book *Wednesday Surprise* with them.)

State the importance of parental involvement in reading by saying, "As parents you are the most influential factor in your child's reading. And since reading is a significant factor in learning and in academic success, your involvement is a powerful predictor of your child's success in the world. That you are here to learn how to encourage your child to read is the first step in doing so—and in ensuring your child's success in the real world."

Sample skill activities: Begin this section by saying, "Let's see how reading can be encouraged. You have already shared insights from the Reading Encouragement Checklist. Now we are going to do a couple of activities that you might want to try at home. As we work through these exercises, I want you to reflect on these questions:
- What did you learn about reading?
- How did the activity facilitate reading?
- How can you encourage reading at home?

Feel free to make comments after each activity, or wait until this portion of the workshop is completed."

Selecting books: This activity shows parents how to choose books for their children. Lead a group discussion on how parents choose books for their children. Record the parents' comments and insights. Illustrate points by showing relevant titles. Add to their ideas by noting the following:
- Children's comments, from library sessions and peer opinions
- Book selection tools such as *Children's Catalog*
- Best book lists (noting that awards do not guarantee child interest)
- Parent guides such as Jim Trelease's *Read-Aloud Handbooks* or the *New York Times Guide to Children's Reading*
- Book store recommendations (being mindful that parent appeal is not the same as child interest)

Suggest that a good book has
- Good plot and characterization
- Positive theme or message
- High quality illustrations (if a picture book)
- Nonsexist and nonracist perspective; avoids stereotypes
- Good binding

It appeals to your child's interests and challenges your child to read at a higher level.

Tell the parents some good ways to buy books for their child:
- School library book fairs
- Public library book fairs
- School book clubs
- Commercial book clubs
- Bookstores that act as children's reading advocates

Remind parents that award-winners aren't always the best choices, that bookstores and book clubs don't have comprehensive collections, and that the final judge of a book's quality and appropriateness is the child. You may want to create a selection guide sheet from the above points.

Reading with your child: Model a reading session by sharing a book aloud with parents. Simulate the family experience by having them sit closely and casually around you as you present the book. Discuss their response to the reading session. Synthesize their responses. Offer the following generalizations, perhaps in a guide sheet, about reading aloud to children:
• Sit close to the child.
• Let the child see the pictures and share the words with you.
• Short, frequent reading sessions are better than occasional long-winded sessions.
• Pace the story and vary your voice to hold interest.
• Read the entire book, or stop at an exciting climax point.
• Stop reading if the book is degrading, boring, or inaccurate.
• Allow time for the child to reflect and respond to the book.
• Share insights and responses.

Processing: Have each group reflect on the activity by answering the questions posed at the start of the session. Report their comments.

Break: Suggest that this time might be well spent examining book displays and parent shelves, since the next activity will be to construct a resource list of useful parent titles.

Resources: Hand out a sample bibliography of parent sources for potential use at home. Show some titles that might otherwise be overlooked and suggest ways to use them at home.

Activity planning: Divide the large group into thirds and have them plan an activity with their children that will encourage reading. The groups may want to brainstorm a number of activities, but they should plan one activity in detail. Give them 20 minutes to summarize and record their plan and discuss the process they followed. They will then report to the large group. The resulting records may be typed up and distributed as a follow-up handout.

Wrap-up: Summarize insights that the participants gained from planning ways to encourage reading at home. Each parent should walk away with at least one usable idea.

Be sure the group is given at least five minutes to evaluate the workshop. This helps in planning future workshops.

In closing, thank all the facilitators and participants.

Resources   Annotated bibliographies of parent sources held by the library. The International Reading Association has good pamphlets.

Evaluation   Each small group shares one idea for encouraging reading. The ideas may be typed up for follow-up distribution in school publications.

Variations
- Focus on one type of activity: reading aloud, book selection.
- Modify sample activities to match different age levels of children.

Reading Encouragement Checklist

Directions: Check those activities you do to encourage your child's reading.

Do you:

- ☐ Read to your child?
- ☐ Read for your own enjoyment?
- ☐ Teach your child nursery rhymes and alphabet songs?
- ☐ Listen to your child read?
- ☐ Talk about reading with your child?
- ☐ Relate stories to real-life experiences?
- ☐ Choose books with your child at the public library?
- ☐ Have your child attend children's programs at the public library?
- ☐ Buy your child books?
- ☐ Subscribe to children's magazines?
- ☐ Let your child choose books or magazines?
- ☐ Establish quiet times and places for home reading?
- ☐ Provide reading-related activities, such as reading games, shopping, doing activities that involve reading directions, or writing?
- ☐ Stimulate your child's interests by visiting museums, parks, and historic sites?
- ☐ Encourage book exchanges between friends?
- ☐ Provide audiocassette versions of books?
- ☐ Build links between television watching and reading?

Notes

Bibliography

Acheson, Keith A., and Meredith D. Gall, *Techniques in the Clinical Supervision of Teachers*, 2nd ed. New York: Longman, 1987.

Allen, Christine, ed., *Skills for Life: Library Information Literacy for Grades K-6*. Worthington OH: Linworth, 1993.

American Library Association Presidential Commission on Information Literacy, *Final Report*. Chicago: ALA, 1989.

American Library Association and Association for Educational and Communications Technology, *Information Power: Guidelines for School Library Media Programs*. Chicago: ALA, 1988.

Brookfield, Stephen D., *Understanding and Facilitating Adult Learning*. San Francisco: Jossey-Bass, 1986.

Cervero, Ronald M., *Effective Continuing Education for Professionals*. San Francisco: Jossey-Bass, 1988.

Cleaver, Betty and William D. Taylor., *The nstructional Consultant Role of the School Library Media Specialist*. Chicago: ALA, 1989.

Cross, K. Patricia., *Adults as Learners*. San Francisco: Jossey-Bass, 1992.

Cutlip, Glen W., *Learning and Information*. Englewood, CO: Libraries Unlimited, 1988.

Davis, Larry N., and Eral McCallon., *Planning, Conducting, Evaluating Workshops*. Auston: Learning Concepts, 1974.

Eitington, Julius., *The Winning Trainer*. Houston: Gulf, 1984.

Farmer, Lesley S. J., *Cooperative Learning Activities in the Library Media Center*. Englewood CO: Libraries Unlimited, 1991.

Farmer, Lesley S. J., *Creative Partnerships: Librarians and Teachers Working Together*. Worthington OH: Linworth, 1992.

Houle, Cyril O., *The Design of Education*. San Francisco: Jossey-Bass, 1976.

Johnson, David W., and Frank P. Johnson., *Joining Together*. Englewood Cliffs, NJ: Prentice-Hall, 1975.

Joyce, Bruce, ed., *Changing School Culture Through Staff Development.* Alexandria VA: Association for Supervision and Curriculum Development, 1990.

Jweid, R. H., and M. Rizzo., *Library-Classroom Partnership.* Metuchen NJ: Scarecrow, 1988.

Kibbey, Marsha, ed., *Skills for Life: Library Information Literacy for Grades 6-8.* Worthington OH: Linworth, 1993.

Marlan, Michael, *Information Skills in the Reading Curriculum.* Metuchen NJ: Scarecrow, 1981.

Neale, D. R., W. J. Bailey, and B. E. Ross, *Strategies for School Improvement.* Boston: Allyn and Bacon, 1981.

O'Donnell, Peggy, and Julie Virgo, *Continuing Education Plan for California Librarians: A Preliminary Draft.* Sacramento: California State Library, 1991.

Power, Bob, *Instructor Excellence.* San Francisco: Jossey-Bass, 1992.

Rux, Paul, ed., *Skills for Life: Library Literacy for Grades 9-12.* Worthington OH: Linworth, 1993.

Trelease, Jim, *The New Read-Aloud Handbook*, 2nd ed. New York: Penguin Books, 1989.

Turner, Philip M., *Helping Teachers Teach.* 2nd ed. Englewood CO: Libraries Unlimited, 1993.

Vandergrift, Kay E., *Power Teaching: A Primary Role of the School Library Media Specialist.* Chicago: ALA, 1994.

Wehmeyer, Lillian Biremann, *The School Librarian as Educator.* Englewood CO: Libraries Unlimited, 1984.

Wlodkowski, Raymond J., *Enhancing Adult Motivation to Learn.* San Francisco: Jossey-Bass, 1986.

Appendix

Topics for Fact Sheets

Not all subjects are best taught in workshops. For example, technical details on using a CD-ROM product are better taught one-to-one or as a self-based tutorial. Fact sheets offer another means of instruction. Students and teachers can choose the single sheet that meets their specific need, and read it in conjunction with their assignment.

Fact sheets are typical user-driven; that is, they are created in response to frequently asked questions, such as "How do you interpret an entry in *Reader's Guide*?" Fact sheets are also practical because they can be easily updated.

The following list suggests topics that lend themselves to fact sheets. Good sources to consult when producing these fact sheets include the study guide section of encyclopedias, introductory sections of basic reference tools, study guides produced by national news periodicals, Arco and Barron's study guides, English grammar and composition books, and, of course, library skills books.

When creating fact sheets, consider making one set of sheets aimed at students and another directed to teachers. Give a master list of each set to all faculty so they can choose and make copies of individual materials for classroom use as well as for library use.

All Levels:
Library vocabulary
Using audiovisual aids
Evaluation and selection of materials

Primary Level (Grades 1-3):
Simple parts of a book
Simple card catalog use

Intermediate Level (Grades 4-6):
Dictionary use: guide words, parts of an entry
Encyclopedia use
Parts of a book and magazine
Kinds of books
Card catalog
Dewey Decimal System

Middle School Level (Grades 7-9):

Literary genres
Specialized dictionaries use
Almanac use
Simple bibliography citations
Simple magazine index use

High School Level (Grades 10-12):

Subject headings
Index use: general and specialized
Bibliography and footnote citations
Primary and secondary sources
Research strategies

Notes

Notes